Romanced
TO
DEATH

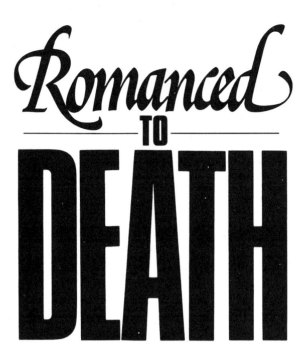

Romanced TO DEATH

The Sexual Seduction Of American Culture

Paul deParrie

Wolgemuth & Hyatt, Publishers, Inc.
Brentwood, Tennessee

The mission of Wolgemuth & Hyatt, Publishers, Inc. is to publish and distribute books that lead individuals toward:

- A personal faith in the one true God: Father, Son, and Holy Spirit;

- A lifestyle of practical discipleship; and

- A worldview that is consistent with the historic, Christian faith.

Moreover, the Company endeavors to accomplish this mission at a reasonable profit and in a manner which glorifies God and serves His Kingdom.

© 1989 by Paul deParrie. All rights reserved
Published March 1990. First Edition
Printed in the United States of America
97 96 95 94 93 92 91 90   8 7 6 5 4 3 2 1

Unless otherwise noted, all Scripture quotations are from the King James Version of the Bible.

Wolgemuth & Hyatt, Publishers, Inc.
1749 Mallory Lane, Suite 110, Brentwood, Tennessee 37027.

Library of Congress Cataloging-in-Publication Data

DeParrie, Paul.
    Romanced to death : the sexual seduction of American culture / Paul deParrie. — 1st ed.
       p   cm.
    ISBN 0-943497-90-6
    1. Sex—Religious aspects—Christianity. 2. United States—Moral conditions. 3. United States—Popular culture. I. Title.
BT708.D46 1990
241'.66—dc20
                                90-30234
                                      CIP

To my one-for-life wife, Bonnie

CONTENTS

INTRODUCTION

T his volume will attempt to trace the sexual revolution in Western civilization back to its innocuous beginning with the changing definitions of *love*
back in the Late Middle Ages, when love changed
from a commitment to being a mere emotional state. I
do not mean to suggest that this is the first time such a
tactic was used. Even the adulterous woman of Proverbs 7 used the insidious device saying, "Let us take
our fill of love" (v. 18, NKJV). But my focus here is
how Western civilization has been sold into sexual
slavery — a spiritual skin trade, if you will.

My tone may seem harsh at times, but it more accurately reflects dismay, especially as regards the
church's acceptance of the precepts of the skin trade. I
approach this as one who was a culturally indoctri-
nated slave of mass sexualization. *Culture blindness* is
an appropriate concept in this regard. We are so inundated in this perversity that we fail to recognize how
distorted our basic assumptions are. After my conversion I became aware of the pervasive influence of the

skin trade in my life, and I deliberately set out to escape the world's mold. This has long been an expected commitment for Christians. I have made some poor choices, but my fervent prayer for escape elicited the mercy of God, and He has continued to forgive and remold me. I approach this work with a certain trepidation since I, of all people, have not stood as a lifelong beacon of the principles I espouse, but am a refugee, a relative newcomer to understanding the effects of Satan's saturation of Western civilization with hedonistic doctrine.

I contend that Satan has been "romancing" the West — romancing us to death.

In this book I have said many negative things about emotions, especially that state of anxiety we call "love." From the outset I would like to say that I am not against emotion. It is a part of God's creation in man and, as such, has a legitimate function — but that function is *not* as a basis for decisions. Certainly, emotions sometimes act as a barometer for our physical state. Some emotions, like love, are wonderfully pleasant and, like all pleasures, it was created by God. It is the *abuse* of God's created pleasure that is sinful. C. S. Lewis pointed out in *Screwtape Letters* that hell has never been able to *create* a new pleasure — only to pervert an existing legitimate one.[1]

I hope this explanation will serve to dissuade people from believing that I must be some dour, gruel-eating killjoy, though I'm sure some will persist in that detraction. A recent experience assures me that this is true.

After speaking at length with a Christian gentleman about the difference between sexual pleasure as a *blessing* as opposed to a *purpose* — and being extremely careful to define my terms — I later came to find that this brother had concluded that I was opposed to women having orgasm! I believe that this and other similar experiences are indicative of how deeply even Christians in the West are sold into the idea that pleasure is a right. But I incorporate copious explanations of what I actually mean by my assertions in the body of this book — and for those who *insist* on misunderstanding, I write this explanation in the introduction and hope it will be read. I feel that enough has been written by others in defense of — and even in exaltation of — emotions and pleasure that I need not repeat the process here.

1

SOLD TO THE SKIN TRADE

The lights of ragged Times Square flashed and reflected off the rain-drenched streets as the fourteen-year-old boy ran frantically from the miserable hotel. He dashed toward the Port Authority bus terminal where nodding junkies were as common as the paper litter that clotted every corner and the lights burned daylight-bright, revealing the greasy, gritty coating on everything in sight.

In hot pursuit was the angry pimp who had held the boy captive for six weeks and sold him to passers-by like he would sell pony rides or turns on a video game. "I'll kill you—you . . . ." He uttered a string of profanities as he gestured meaningfully toward the boy with a broken bottle. His longer strides gave him the advantage and he gained on his terrified prey. Uniformed guards for the Port Authority glanced up and then looked away as if seeking something to guard.

The boy sped under the Port Authority skybridge toward a nondescript, tan high-rise several blocks away. It was The Covenant House, a shelter for Times Square's lost youth — prostitutes and drug addicts. He dodged cars and narrowly missed a crushing blow crossing the street, splattering through a curbside puddle of grimy water. There was a light at the gate of Father Ritter's Covenant House. The boy's heart leaped as he crossed the threshold hoarsely panting, unable even to ask for help.

The pimp dropped back angrily into the shadows. There would be other boys. They daily flocked to the Port Authority, alone and bewildered.[1]

        ❧   ❧   ❧

There is urgency in his voice as he leans forward. His skin is pallid. He faces death in a few hours.

"Okay," he tells his interviewer. "But before we go any further, I think it's important to me that people believe what I'm saying. I'm not blaming pornography; I'm not saying that it caused me to go out and do certain things. And I take full responsibility for whatever I've done and all the things that I've done. That's not the question here. The question and the issue is how this kind of literature contributed and helped mold and shape the kinds of violent behavior. . ." His voice seems to falter and he leans back slightly. The interviewer interjects, "It fueled your fantasies."

The faded orange prison garb is flaccid and worn. He seems to consider the statement before continuing. "In the beginning it fuels this kind of thought process," he comments almost as a spectator. But he seems to grow more tense as he says, "Then at a certain time it's instrumental in what I would call crystallizing it — making it into what is almost like a separate entity inside. At that point you're at a verge — or I was at the verge of acting out these kinds of thoughts."

The interviewer asks for clarification and the pale-faced prisoner responds, "I would keep looking for more potent, more explicit, more graphic kinds of materials . . . until you reach the point where pornography only goes so far. You reach that jumping-off point where you begin to wonder if maybe actually doing it will give you that which is beyond just reading about it or looking at it."

The interview proceeds, and the subject seems to alternately become resigned then agitated about the review of his heinous career. His intensity grows under the fatal deadline of tomorrow and the scrutiny of the questioner.

"There is just absolutely no way to describe . . . ," he says and then hesitates. "First the brutal urge to do that kind of thing and then what happens. I want people to understand this too, and I'm not saying this gratuitously, because it's important that people understand this. That, basically, I was a normal person. I wasn't some guy hanging out in bars or a bum. Or I wasn't a pervert in the sense that people look at somebody and say, 'I know there's something wrong with him; I can just tell.' But I was essentially a normal person. I had good friends. I lived a normal life, except for this one

small, but very potent, very destructive segment that I
kept very secret — very close to myself — and I didn't
let anybody know about it."[2]

ﻻ   ﻻ   ﻻ

"We will sodomize your sons," wrote militant homosexual Michael Swift, jeering at the heterosexual
culture, "emblems of your feeble masculinity, of your
shallow dreams and vulgar lies. We shall seduce them
in your schools, in your dormitories, in your gymnasiums . . . wherever men are with men together. Your
sons will become our minions and do our bidding.
They will be recast in our image. They will come to
crave and adore us."[3]

ﻻ   ﻻ   ﻻ

A six-year-old La Crosse, Wisconsin boy who
forced other children to remove their clothes and touch
each other has been charged with sexual assault and
ordered out of his mother's custody.

According to police files, the boy reportedly met
children in a wooded area near the apartment complex
where he lived and would show them pictures of nude
women and tell the other children to remove their
clothes and touch each other. When some of the children refused, the boy forcibly removed their pants.[4]

ﻻ   ﻻ   ﻻ

The pornographer had sent three henchmen out to
find a "product" — a young blonde to star in his latest
movie. When the men were unable to find a willing
subject, Johnny Zinn, the boss, said, "Okay, you will
just have to grab someone off the street."

The three roamed the streets until they spotted Linda Daniels, a twenty-two-year-old college student, pulling into a grocery store lot. "There — that's the one we want — the boss likes blondes."

When she completed her shopping, they followed her home and grabbed her from the driveway, gagged her with a bandanna, bound her hands with wire, and took her to a motel where she was repeatedly raped and photographed. But Zinn knew she could identify them and ordered his cohorts to "get rid of her."

Linda was taken to the mountains where she was shot.[5]

               ❧   ❧   ❧

All of these stories and many more have happened in modern America. What could have happened to a civilization that was based on Christian morals? How did such sexual barbarity spring up in our midst? What went wrong?

I contend that we have been sold into sexual slavery — but before that, we had sexual slavery sold *to* us.

The Sale of the Millennia — New Morals for Old

"Prices Slashed! These Items Must Go!" These words jump out of the newsprint at you and there it is! The very thing you've been needing and were unable to afford. Indeed, the prices *have* been slashed. *At this price,* you think, *I can actually afford it.*

You swing into your car, coax the hesitant engine to start, and rumble down the street to take advantage of the sale. Walking briskly, you enter the store and head for the proper department. Scanning the shelves, you don't see your item. *Perhaps it is at the end of an aisle on display*, you think. But the search proves fruitless, so you snag a scurrying employee and explain your dismay.

"Yes, sir," he says politely. "We're completely out of those — but maybe I could interest you in this other brand. Actually, this one has many advantages over the one you wanted. For instance . . ."

ꙮ   ꙮ   ꙮ

It is an old technique. A business uses an ad for some product in limited stock as bait to draw customers. When the small stock is sold, the salesmen try to switch the target's attention to another, more expensive product. They know that the customer has already set it in his mind to buy the item, and most people find it easier to buy the substitute than to wait for the "real thing."

The technique is called *bait-and-switch*. The object is to distract the customer from his original intent. I believe "love" has been used as the bait to draw Christian civilization from its Rock onto the mucky bogs of the world. But more than that, we are being sold into slavery and prostitution by the process.

Few realize that the advertising industry is *not* about selling products as much as it is about selling *people*. Television stations do not make their livelihood by selling Cheer or a Chevrolet to you but by selling *you* to the companies that buy the airtime. That's why it is so important for them to have ratings — not to see which show is popular and respond to viewers but to know how many people they are hawking to the makers of Jell-O or Jeep.

The *Bait* — the Love Myth

The sales campaign I am referring to in this book, however, did not originate on Madison Avenue (though the campaign has its full cooperation) but in the boardrooms of hell. The *bait*, in this case is "love" — or rather I should say, a new definition of love: love presented as a *feeling*. This is the Love Myth. I am not necessarily only referring to love in the romantic sense, though that occupies the lion's share of Satan's sales strategy in this day. Though the love of family, country, church, or anything else would be destroyed if diminished to only feeling, love in the romantic sense is the most potent weapon in Satan's advertising arsenal. The success of this advertising venture is measured, in hell's terms, by the prostitution and enslavement of the people in Western society. As with Madame Babylon in Revelation 17 – 18, the merchandise is the "bodies and souls of men" (18:13, NKJV). Satan is the procurer in the skin trade.

The *skin trade* has been a designation for both prostitution and slavery. Often in the past the two were closely connected. I believe civilization has been sold into sexual slavery and prostitution, and that is evidenced by the moral condition of this country. The free-sex, gay-rights atmosphere of today testifies to an entirely new (at least in America) view of family, marriage, and sex. This is not to say that I particularly believe in some "golden age" when everyone believed the same things and behaved in a civilized manner, for, as long as man has been man-out-of-the-Garden, he has corrupted God's order in these things. There *was*, however, a time when most Americans accepted Biblical teachings on marriage, family, and sex as the normal thing. Aberrations were hidden and relatively rare. Now marriage is for love (the *feeling*, not the commitment), and the purpose of sex is pleasure.

Am I saying that feelings and emotions are wrong? No. Do I think that pleasure in marital sex is sin? Not at all. But emotions have a specific place in life and it is *not* in the driver's seat. And pleasure, though a blessing from God, is not the *reason* God created sex. Once these simple distinctions were commonly understood. Now we are so inundated in this feeling-and-sex-oriented culture that we react almost instinctively against the suggestion that too much emphasis is placed on either emotion or sexual pleasure.

Malcolm Muggeridge tells of evidence of the importance of sex to our culture when describing the public ordeal of one of the early heart transplant recipients.

> Only three weeks after he had received his new heart, he was able to tell an expectant world that he

had succeeded in having sexual intercourse. It was the twentieth-century certification of being fully alive: *copulo ergo sum*.[6]

What happened to the seemingly obvious positions on marriage and family? How did we go from a culture that held marriage and family so highly that divorced people were viewed as deviations, where adulterers were considered untrustworthy, where a child molester would have been executed, to a society that features these things as topics of light conversation on afternoon TV talk shows? Why is it when the church tries to respond intelligently to these things, that the warning has an unsure sound? We were looking for love, but what we got in the *switch* of the bait-and-switch was a perversion of all of the good things God has created in marriage and sex.

The *Switch* — Sexual Perversion

I believe that America, including the church, has been seduced with lies and flatteries that have undermined all connections to a solid, Biblical basis for the important subjects of family, marriage, and sex. G. K. Chesterton once observed that in order to change a nation's religion, one only needed to change its language. Such has been the case in Western civilization. The change has not been sudden, but it has been subtle. In fact, all the Christian virtues — compassion, courage, peace, patience — have suffered together the ignominy of being reduced to feelings. "One of the sexual addict's biggest

problems," says Steve Gallagher of Pure Life Ministries, "is the fact that he is *feeling* oriented, rather than
being obedience oriented."[7] The same Love Myth that
unsaved Americans bought and that has enslaved them
in a sexual Disneyland has prostituted the gospel of
Jesus Christ and made it impotent against the hedonistic flood. It no longer seems to matter if someone per-
forms acts of compassion — it matters if they *feel* compassion. But the most destructive of Satan's tools has
been the distortion of love.

Revelation 18 describes that great "mother of harlots," Madame Babylon, and tells of her traffic in the
"bodies and souls of men" (v. 13, NKJV). She is the
prostitutor of the world, and her agents, the societal
pimps, are ever marketing their pandering philoso-
phies. Wrapped in the cloak of proper psychology, respectable reasoning, and suitable scientific studies, this
insidious, ignominious instruction burrows into the
core of our ideas from whence it diffuses throughout
our lives and culture.

Most of Western civilization is now captured by
the curious and patently unscriptural notions that the
purpose of marriage is "love" and the purpose of sex is
pleasure. These are direct consequences of the false
idea that love is an emotion rather than a commitment.
In this generation, the simplicity of *God's* purpose in
marriage, family, and sex has so long been neglected
that it is now despised as archaic. Few know or care to
find out the reasons and Scripture behind the earlier
teachings on these subjects. In truth, most Christians

are inordinately proud of the "progress" the church has made in these areas—the "openness," the "honesty," and the "transparency" on sexual subjects. Yet, the fruit of all this openness has been an increase in divorce, illegitimate pregnancy, abortion, adultery, homosexuality, and pornography use in the church—almost to the level of the unsaved world and sometimes surpassing it.

Some would contend that these things were always so, only they were hypocritically submerged. But no evidence bears this out, only the bitter jealousies of the societal pimps who would have us believe that true faith in Jesus Christ makes not one whit of difference. I, however, beg to differ. And, furthermore, I believe it is possible to extricate ourselves from this cultural prostitution with the help of that same Jesus Christ.

What We Have Seen

- Western civilization has been sold into sexual slavery and prostitution—the *skin trade*.

- The marketing technique called *bait-and-switch* was used to accomplish this.

- The *bait* was "love," a love which was presented as an emotion rather than a commitment—a Love Myth.

- What civilization received in the *switch* was the profane forms of sex.

- Satan was the author of this advertising campaign.

- Modern psychology and sociology have strongly supported the Love Myth.

- The acceptance of the Love Myth has led to the twin unscriptural conclusions that the purpose of marriage is "love" and the purpose of sex is pleasure.

- The widespread, but often subliminal, dependence on the Love Myth has led to the shattering of Christian marriage and the flourishing of every form of sexual perversion.

- It is possible to recover the Scriptural view and purpose of marriage and sex.

What We Will See

In the next chapter we will look at the pattern of seduction as described in Scripture and the same bait-and-switch technique that I have explained in this chapter.

In Proverbs, there are several general descriptions of temptation which will correspond to the stories of Samson, David, Solomon, and Joseph. Those who avoided sin were preserved by God's grace. But, of those who bought the bait, *none* got what they thought they were getting. Of those who did not quickly repent, *all* ended up as merchandise in Satan's skin trade.

2

THE SCRIPTURES AND SEDUCTION

To me, she stood out in glaring relief. She wore blue jeans and a tank-top T-shirt, and she virtually hugged the bus stop. It could have been any modern girl standing there holding the small purse, awaiting the rumbling, orange city bus.

"Working tonight, eh?" my wife Bonnie commented to no one in particular as we drove past the girl standing by the squalid boulevard.

Our passenger gave a little "Huh?" and perked up. "*She's* a prostitute? How can you tell?"

"Well," I began, "a lot of them dress for the job. But even when they don't, they are easy to spot once you know what to look for."

We passed a few more obvious prostitutes as if to accentuate my point. The boarded-up buildings provided a dull background for their often flamboyant plumage.

"It's in the eyes," Bonnie added. "They are always searching the people driving by—hoping to make eye contact, hoping to catch them by their eyes with *the look.*"

When we first volunteered for the street outreach, it had only taken a couple of visits to the depressing strip to learn this. How true the warning from Proverbs 6:25: "Lust not after her beauty in thine heart; neither let her take thee with her eyelids." For indeed, it was often *the look* that was integral to the snare.[1]

ঌ   ঌ   ঌ

I don't think I would find much argument if I were to say that America has become sexually hyperactive— nor if I asserted that where we stand (or more accurately, *sink*) today is the result of a step-by-step regression from a more self-controlled time. Our path to this condition could easily be described as a seduction. The bleats of the media proclaim both their near hysteria over rising teen pregnancy rates and their tawdry fixation with sexual deviancy. The same issues of magazines and newspapers will bellow denunciations of rape and the exploitation of women and children, while displaying obscene amounts of women's flesh like so much flank steak—all for the purpose of peddling wrenches or automobiles. Children are posed in sultry, sexual settings with unnatural leers distorting their faces. All seem to have *the look.* Liberal publications, normally sensitive to exploitation, print fashion ads that verge on suggesting nymphomania. Internationally acclaimed perfumers' messages include dark hints of homosexuality, lesbianism, orgies, and oedipal relationships. No one balks.

This prostitution of America did not come overnight. But, in order to understand seduction, I believe we must turn to God's Word. I am convinced that the essentials of seduction are the same whether applied individually or culturally. The first element we will address is *the look.*

The Look

In the vignette at the start of the chapter, the first contact of the prostitute was through eye contact — a powerful means of getting someone's attention. The idea is to snag the passerby's consciousness and convey an intensely salacious message simultaneously. Herein is the bait — the intensely delivered promise of "love" or "romance." It would be impossible to overestimate the role that this kind of fantasy plays in seduction. In fact, if the imagination of the person is not captured, the seduction will fail.

Also, we need to remember that it is not only the bait but the carnal nature in man which rises to the bait that completes the transaction. Scripture is explicit that "men loved darkness rather than light" (John 3:19), so sin is not the product of the tempter alone. E. C. S. Gibson puts it this way in his commentary on James: "A man sins only when he is 'enticed' by the bait, and 'drawn away' by the hook of 'his own lust.'"2

But that first suggestion of a thought is not a sinful act if it is not entertained. Jesus indicated that looking at a woman to lust after her was the line of demarcation that constituted adultery (see Matthew 5:28). And it is not always necessary for someone to actually participate for the deleterious effects to be felt. Simple tolerance will be enough. Even though the passerby in the above example may refuse to engage in lustful thoughts, he has certainly received the message that sex is available at that particular corner. If he does nothing and he sees her out there day after day, especially if there appears to be no police response, the message becomes: *This kind of thing is normal and acceptable.* If he then sees her often going with customers, the message changes to: *There must be something good or right in this.* If the prostitute lives in the area and the passerby sees her at the store or dropping her child at day-care, she becomes "just an ordinary girl trying to make ends meet." Certainly we can see how even this person's thoughts have been captured, starting with *the look.*

Thus neighborhoods eventually succumb to the seemingly inevitable transition to becoming "that part of town." This steady decline is also visible on the moral landscape. If one is honest, he realizes that both the hooker and her customer are prostitutes, for both are distorting and perverting God's order. But the person who knows better and is *tolerant* has been the silent partner to the societal pimp.

Yet "that part of town," whether physical or moral, has a unique vitriol — a pandemic infestation which rots the posts and beams of society's frame. This is the switch end of the deal. A neighborhood thinks that "love" is for sale, when it is really *it* that is being sold.

The grave, repeated warnings in Proverbs expose that the first tools of the prostitute and the prostitutor — much like the advertiser — are smooth words (see Proverbs 5:3). Once the *attention* of society is caught by some subtle, smoldering sensuality, the smooth words begin to flow, attempting to cloak the tawdry suggestions with an aura of beauty like the caked-on makeup of the brazen hooker. The come-on must disguise the seaminess with sentimentality or some other desirable aspect. Again we see the role of fantasy.

With the smooth words the hook is set. The victim wriggles and thrashes ineffectually but, like the analogous fish, has no comprehension of what he struggles against. So a society lured by a fleeting glance at open sexuality and snared by the smooth words of "love," "romance," and "beauty" instinctively resists but is unsure of how to frame its resistance. In the face of powerful forces like emotion and lust, Scripture and reason both seem cold and sterile.

The Lure of Lust

"Therefore came I forth to meet *thee*," the adulteress in Proverbs 7 says boldly, "diligently to seek *thy* face, and I have found *thee*," she adds intoxicatingly[3] as she clutches him and brazenly kisses him. The snare is sprung with blinding speed, and the foolish young man is held hypnotized by her blandishments. She extols her offerings.

"Let us take our fill of love," she whispers enticingly in a blatant bait-and-switch over the meaning of "love." But he is oblivious to the scam. "Let us solace ourselves with loves," she urges.

Her deadly delights are lusciously described as the wares of the great cosmopolitan cultures of the time. Sophisticated sensual pleasures of artistry and exotic smells and spices are the trappings of her offerings. And besides, she adds, no one else will know; her husband is gone and won't be back for a long time.

The rest of the passage defines the foolish young man's decline. The entire incident can serve as a template for a society that is being prostituted, enslaved by the lure of "love," and being, as the foolish young man, led "as an ox"[4] to the sheer walls of hell.

Look carefully at the description. There seems to be an initial hesitancy on the young man's part, but the continuous use of "fair speech" and flattery wears down his resistance. But the very fact that the foolish young man was in the part of town inhabited by prostitutes shows a flaw in his defenses. Perhaps he had seen *the look* there earlier, and his fantasy life had been working ever since. And it is this flaw that the prostitute exploits when "he goeth after her straightway, as an ox goeth to the slaughter" (v. 22). From this point there seems to be no impediment to his downward journey until "a dart strike through his liver" (v. 23). Here he finally realizes the switch. In Biblical times, a puncture of the liver, or any of the viscera, was deadly — slowly and painfully deadly. The wounded person knew he was dying, but there was nothing that could be done for him. In the same way, eventually the foolish young man sustained a fatal wound from his "romance" with prostitutes. With horror, he realized how he had come to this pass, but there would be no remedy. "He, that being often reproved hardeneth his neck, shall suddenly be destroyed, and that without remedy" (Proverbs 29:1). The cup of sin is full, and God's judgment becomes apparent; it is too late; he is "brought to a piece of bread" (Proverbs 6:26); his own soul is destroyed.

Proverbs also says that the prostitute "will hunt for the *precious* life" (6:26, emphasis added). I believe this indicates that these temptations are particularly aimed at men and women to whom God has given special work. The last two verses of Proverbs 7 reveal more about this adulterous woman: "For she hath cast down many wounded: yea, many strong men have been slain by her. Her house is the way to hell, going down to the chambers of death."

The Samson Syndrome

Samson had no particular business in Timnath; it had just been a whim to go there. The mideastern sun was high in the cloudless sky, and the breeze swayed the tender wheat stalks. Samson headed for the town well for a drink, and as he approached he noticed a particularly attractive maiden who stood under an awning near the square.

She had raven hair that was plaited in long, looped braids intertwined with golden strands. Her eyes sparkled as she laughed at some secret joke with her friends. Her neck was long and smooth. He *had* to have her. Samson could hardly contain his excitement as he bounded home to beg his parents to get her for him.

Samson was a man set apart, holy to the Lord — a Nazirite. He was the miracle child of a barren womb. He was a strong man — like the target of the Proverbs' prostitute.

Despite his prophetic origins, Samson was a man with a decided lack of self-control. Samson was in love with love — the glandular, emotional reaction — and insisted on marrying the Philistine princess. He followed his own feelings into the relationship. The mere sight of this woman was enough for Samson to abandon the prohibitions of God (see Judges 14:1–3). No Israelite was to marry a foreign woman, and Nazirites, like Samson, were called to a uniquely stringent separation.

There is no record that Samson's parents were somehow inept or culpable, but Samson still managed to base his life on his senses — the true sensual man.

Some will undoubtedly argue that Scripture declares that the Lord used this inordinate relationship to spark a rejoinder against the uncircumcised nation of the Philistines. But that fact, by itself, does not justify Samson's lust, for it is this same fatal flaw that finally destroys him. The ultimate plan of the seducer, in this case, failed, but that does not ameliorate Samson's actions.

Rather than turn from his inordinate love, though, Samson continued his headlong plunge. He was now entirely blinded. After the loss of his Philistine bride, he continued in submission to emotional sensuality and embraced the visceral pleasures of a prostitute (see Judges 16:1–3). As with the Philistine's daughter, the harlot was the source of serious subsequent problems. In the former, he had created a situation in which, had it not been for God's intervention and sovereign plan, he would have been killed. This, however, did nothing to dissuade Samson from foolishly endangering his own life again when he was hooked by the prostitute.

All of the miraculous intervention in Samson's life did not save him from his own foolishness. He was first enticed into an ungodly marriage, later snared by a prostitute, and finally caught in Delilah's subterfuge that led to death. The warnings of Proverbs come quickly to mind.

Samson's uncontrolled "love" for Delilah blinded him to her covert mission of destruction (see Judges 16:4–20). Anyone but a fool should have been able to discern the subversive nature of her acts. But such is the nature of lust. He was sold into slavery by the combination of his desire and his undisciplined "love."

He was led "as an ox," like the foolish young man of Proverbs 7 to his dreary fate. He had been prostituted. His God-given strength had been perverted from God's service against the Philistine oppression of Israel to the grinding mills feeding the uncircumcised, a graphic illustration of Proverbs 5:8-11:

> Remove thy way far from her, and come not nigh the door of her house: lest thou give thine honour unto others, and thy years unto the cruel: lest strangers be filled with thy wealth; and thy labours be in the house of a stranger; and thou mourn at the last, when thy flesh and thy body are consumed.

Of course, the most obvious warning here is that one should be especially careful to guard against "minor" deviations from God's Word. But the real hook in Samson's life was his willingness to make so important a decision as marriage based on his glandular/emotional state.

Obviously such a base is ultimately selfish. After all, Samson's decisions were dependent on how they made *him* feel — to the exclusion of God, his parents, or, for that matter, the women involved. Sin appealed to Samson's selfish tendencies, just as the adulteress in Proverbs 7 appealed to the foolish young man's. Only when Samson was finally captured, did he realize his folly. But it was too late. Like the slow, sure death from an abdominal wound, his wages were the protracted agony of slavery, blindness, and the knowledge that God intended better for him had he not squandered his heritage.

At the last, Samson was a slave — a blue-ribbon exhibit in the skin trade auction. He had been *romanced to death.*

David's Deviation

It was spring. The wildflowers were beginning to carpet the rocky hills of Moriah around Jerusalem. David was securely placed as king. The land was his.

But there were still the border raids. Ammonites, swarming from their nest in Rabbah across the river, plagued the frontier, and people called to King David for relief. Spring was the time of year for him to put on his kingly armor and lead his warriors into the fray. It was also the ideal time strategically to corner the vast majority of the Ammonite culprits while they were still in Rabbah.

But David was king, and he didn't *feel* like a protracted, muddy, bloody campaign in the wastes east of the river. *Sure, my men fight better when I am there,* he thought. *But they'll do all right under Joab. I need a vacation from all this responsibility.*

David stood in a casual robe overlooking his departing troops. The shields and bucklers reflected the noonday sun and clattered together as the formations moved through the city gates. By sunset the column finally disappeared from sight. Only the dust cloud raised by thousands of marching feet marked their po-

sition. But David had since gone to bed. He tossed fit-
fully, sleep escaped him, and restlessness finally drove
him back to the roof.

David enjoyed the sun's heat, which was finally
reaching his bones after the unusually bitter winter. He
strolled along the parapet surveying the city in the rapidly dwindling twilight. There was the plot where the
future temple would be built. *A temple of my design,*
he thought to himself as he ambled to the northern end
of the roof.

Looking down across the flat rooftops of Jerusalem, he saw a beautiful woman bathing between two
lampstands. No natural recoil drew his eyes away;
rather he took special note that her beauty was extraordinary. *"I wonder who she is?"* he asked himself.

The trap was sprung.

ﻮ   ﻮ   ﻮ

David had it made — and that was the problem. The
relative calm of his life at this time lulled him into
self-centeredness. The Scripture does not tell us exactly
why David stayed behind, but it makes it clear that he
was shirking responsibility when he did (see 2 Samuel
11). Perhaps he reasoned that the weight of kingly responsibilities he had borne at home gave him the right
to choose his time off. He may have argued that he
could hardly be a proper king if he did not take care of
himself. Maybe his counselors agreed. In any event, it
is clear that this was a deviation in his normal acceptance of duty.

But it was enough. David's highlighted position in God's plan made minor slips particularly damaging. After all, God had said David was a man after His own heart; this made him an irresistible target for the seducer. David's apparent idleness was a contributing factor, but willful pride and self-satisfaction were certainly major forces. David obviously felt that his newly-secured rank entitled him to do pretty much as he pleased. It wasn't enough, as God pointedly reminded later, that he had been *given* the kingdom, Saul's household as a household of his own, and that God would have given him nearly anything else besides.

It was not just the vision of Bathsheba, but David's choice to linger over it and then to allow his thoughts to be engaged by the sight that constituted the sin. Did he imagine he was in love, or was it pure physical lust? Did he excuse the lingering gaze saying he was merely admiring the beauty of the human form? Or did he imagine she was essential to some emotional need? It matters little—the results are all the same. By the time David ordered an inquiry into her identity, he was probably completely spiritually blinded and groping his way by his feelings. The great tragedy was that his self-deception and self-will were to cost Uriah the Hittite his life.

David's frustrated attempts to evade responsibility for Bathsheba's pregnancy highlighted the true impotence of his power in opposition to God's. Instead of opening David's eyes to his own devious depravity, the failed plans merely led to more desperate measures to cover his sin. The murder of Uriah, though through subterfuge, was David's final cover story. And it seemed to work until the prophet Nathan arrived.

Here is one place where I believe we can get a glimpse of why David was a man after God's own heart. When directly confronted with his wickedness, David instantly calls out to God in repentance — no weaseling, no whining, no equivocating. How very different from his predecessor, Saul, who always sought to mitigate his culpability and negotiate on the terms of repentance.

But even though David repented, the wounds to his life, his family, and his nation remained for his entire reign. The hard-won peace was gone from all three spheres. The price, though, would certainly have been higher had he ordered Nathan struck down, which was in his power to do. At least his repentance saved him from the ignominious degradation of Samson's end.

Fortunately, David's deviation was not rooted in a long-standing character defect, but his slide into sin was rapid and decisive — and costly.

Again, as with Samson, we see the effects listed in Proverbs 5:8-11 in David's life. But we must not overlook the continued *national* agony that resulted from David's lapse of responsibility. With the sword continually unsheathed during David's reign, Israel endured David's bitter fruit.

Direct transgression is by no means the only way that leaders may afflict the masses with their folly. If David had begun to inject all his governmental decisions with a bias that justified adultery, the devastation would have grown geometrically. His personal sins would soon have been magnified as national sins.

And what would entice a man like David, who had everything and could have had more, to snatch away another man's wife and his life? The only answer I can glean from the text was an enormous swelling of pride. He *could* do it; therefore, he *would* do it. His pride left him heedless of others, heedless of wise counsel, and heedless of God's Word—a fool in the first degree. Proverbs tells us that fools hate instruction and think they know it all (see, for example, 1:7). This is where David's pride took him.

Solomon's Slippery Slope

Jerusalem grew in splendor under Solomon. The city had been nothing unique under the embattled reign of David, but it flourished into a jewel under David's son. The utterly stunning magnificence of the temple crowned the walled fortress. Nothing like it existed in the known world. Solomon's palace was unrivaled in richness and artistry. Even the doors to the stables were hinged with gold.

But it wasn't just the splendor of the city itself that drew the world to its gates, it was the Word of God. Solomon had been blessed with uncanny wisdom and the world was awestruck. Great men and women endured arduous pilgrimages to hear the wis-

dom of God spoken through Solomon (see 1 Kings
4:29–34; 10:1–13).

Solomon, however, was both pragmatic and romantic. He made an alliance with the Pharaoh of Egypt,
sealing it with marriage to Pharaoh's daughter (see 1
Kings 3:1). Such alliances, though, were as anathema
as were marriages to foreign wives. But Solomon
loved his Egyptian bride, loved her enough to build her
a private, luxurious palace, and perhaps used the alliance as a justification for the ill-conceived marriage
(9:24).

But Solomon's "love" was his bane. He fell for it
again and again until he had a collection of foreign
wives and concubines. Solomon, like Samson, was in
love with love. And the corrosive power of that emotional state ate at his resistance to evil. It began with
one forbidden love, justified by political expediency,
and ended in a morass of loves and the burning of in-
cense to cruel Canaanite gods. His lowered personal
resistance to sin softened him with regard to those he
loved. Soon idols appeared in their rooms for personal
devotions. Then he allowed shrines to be built in the
palace and on the grounds. Later, because he "loved"
them, he joined their rites — even to the child-slaughter-
ing Molech (see 1 Kings 11:1-8).

The anger of God smouldered against Solomon,
and the kingdom was eventually rent asunder because
of his sins. All the wisdom that God gave Solomon
was useless without obedience. When emotions re-

ceived higher authority than the Word of God, disaster was imminent.

One contributing factor in Solomon's downfall appears to have been age. For it was in his old age when his most serious breeches occurred.[5] He may have simply grown weary of well-doing and of resisting the pleas of his wives. His marriages to them were the inch that allowed Satan to take the mile.

Joseph's Judgment

"Ps-s-st! Hey, slow down!" he said, looking up from the sign he was working on. "There's no hurry. We're not in a race here."

I looked at the older man briefly, then bent back over my work and continued laying in the letter strokes. We were painting trail signs for the city parks bureau. I understood the hidden meaning of his whispered comment. He meant, "Don't produce a lot of signs. It makes others — particularly myself — look bad."

This is one of two typical American responses to a productive worker. He is either viewed as a threat because of possible comparisons between him and his fellow employees, or the others will allow the productive worker to pick up their slack and take group credit for increased productivity.

Joseph experienced both. He was a faithful man whom his father entrusted with a certain amount of oversight of his brothers' shepherding. His brothers were not kindly disposed to having the youngest in this

place of favor and their resentment seethed. They finally disposed of Joseph. Later, while Joseph was in
prison, the warden simply took advantage of Joseph's
industrious nature and faithfulness by placing him in
charge of the entire prison (see Genesis 37; 39–40).

In a strange way, it was Joseph's very faithfulness
that put him into prison in the first place. When he first
arrived in Egypt, his diligence soon paved a way to the
chief steward position in Potiphar's house. Potiphar and
his household prospered immensely under Joseph's direction. But Potiphar's wife, a wealthy, bored libertine, had
other ideas. Over and over she sought Joseph out to seduce him. Over and over he remained faithful to God and
to Potiphar. Finally, Potiphar's wife made an embarrass-
ingly bold lunge for Joseph. Again Joseph resisted. He
fled the scene of the seduction (see Genesis 39).

Now, some have hinted that perhaps Joseph was in
the wrong place, but Scripture gives no such indica-
tion. Remembering that Joseph's charge included the
entire house, he would have naturally had duties everywhere.

The fact remains, however, that Joseph's long-
standing practice of faithfulness protected him from
something *worse* than imprisonment — namely, the
foreboding destiny of the young man in Proverbs.

An Overview of Samson, David, Solomon, and Joseph

In comparing these examples to the Proverbs texts, the
first thing we might note is that sometimes seduction

seemed to be a matter of a woman's design, as with Delilah and Potiphar's wife, and other times it was men's internal drive, as with David and Solomon. These differences would only be significant to our study if we were asserting that seduction was a *human* plot. It is not.

Seduction of this sort is the product of spiritual warfare against God and His people. Satan is the pimp! It matters not to him whether he leads people by their own internal moral defects or uses an external lure. So, even though Bathsheba may have been unaware (and she probably was) of her alluring composure toward David, David's own unguarded drives were enough. Conversely, Potiphar's wife deliberately set out to snare Joseph. But it is unlikely that either David or Potiphar's wife recognized the underlying strategy of the spiritual pimp, Satan.

If someone has a lot to lose in the sexual affair, it seems to have little or no effect on his or her susceptibility to seduction. David certainly risked all for a little illicit pleasure. And it was only the grace of God that limited the evil reaping. When reading of that dark harvest, which lasted the rest of his days, one shudders to imagine what may have happened if that grace were lacking.

The drive of lust has an imperative that is lacking in the faint warnings of potential loss and that will not be quelled by the satisfactions and lawful pleasures of licit love. It was not simply sex that David's corrupt desire sought but *stolen* pleasure. "Stolen waters are sweet," Proverbs 9:17 says. Thus the fallen nature craves the forbidden, the dangerous, the daring. Perhaps this explains the great danger of edging toward the "small sins." The thrill of danger and the apparent lack of retribution drive men on to further and further risk, winding up in total degeneracy.

Surely Samson is a prime example of how a habitual lack of self-control can pave an expressway of sin. In the other corner is Joseph, a man of *practiced* faithfulness who withstood the combined assault of sex, money, and power—all of which would have been his in abundance for the bedding of his master's wife. But long before the pen of Paul the Apostle scrawled the admonition, Joseph had learned to "flee fornication" (1 Corinthians 6:18).

Samson, on the other hand, didn't stand a chance. He had never practiced self-control, or at least he regarded it as an expendable virtue.

Still, we look at David, a man of tremendous faithfulness and self-control. His early behavior toward Saul—even when Saul sought his life—bears this out. David's life had been rigorous. But just when it seemed that his life had come to a more placid place, David let his guard down—*just once!* And a tragic *once* it was. As a seasoned warrior, he should have been more wary.

Even the special dispensation of Solomon's wisdom was not proof against the corrosive influences of a small compromise. Song of Solomon 2:15 says that it is the little foxes that spoil the vine, and so it was for

Solomon. Great gifts and majesty from God still require faithful maintenance.

Modern Times

The examples of the fallen are by no means limited to the tumultuous tales of the Scripture, the dark events of past peoples. Newspapers gleefully report the failures of Christian notables. But casual excuses that there have always been such men in ministry or that "they are *only* human, after all" are as bogus as the world's cynical assertion that the rigorous repression demanded by religion *causes* such deviation.[6]

Embarrassing revelations of infidelity in firebrand preacher Jimmy Swaggart rocked the American Christian world, long noted for its inordinate idolatry of men. This Famous Personality Syndrome led to denials from "Swaggartites," as well as from swarms of smug aficionados of Jim and Tammy Bakker. The grossest denial was in overlooking the seriousness of the offenses.

Meanwhile, the Swaggart/Bakker soap opera was quietly eclipsed in Virginia where the three top men in the Tony Leyva Evangelistic Association pled guilty to using their sawdust trail as a slave/prostitution transport route for young boys and also guilty to sexually abusing the boys. Dozens of papers in the U.S. report incest and child molestation trials of ministers while a sordid cadre of atheists, humanists, and pagans dance

about saying, "See! See! We told you so!" Then a collection of ministers appeared on the Geraldo Rivera
Show demanding a "sexual bill of rights" allowing
ministers the liberty to be involved in pornography,
homosexuality, and other perversions. The church in
America reels.

But the point is that this odious situation did not
arise in a vacuum. There were times when the church
was considerably cleaner and when such offenses
would have signaled the preparation of tar and feath-
ers. However, the moral decay in the church is liable to
grow worse if remedial steps are not taken to eradicate
the foundational lies upon which this evil trafficking of
human bodies and souls stands. That done, we must
rediscover and don the cloak of righteousness and the
full armor of God with godly perceptions of the function of sex and marriage.

The Principle of Lust

Scripture clearly teaches that lust is born in every child
of Adam. And although it takes different appearances
for men and women, the essential drive is the same.
But, as James states, temptation must first lay hold of
our *innate* lust, then we must surrender to its call for
sin to be conceived. From that point, lust can take on a
life of its own and a power unimaginable. "But every
man is tempted, when he is drawn away of his own
lust, and enticed. Then when lust hath conceived, it

bringeth forth sin: and sin, when it is finished, bringeth forth death" (James 1:14–15).

As noted before, lust is not a rational drive that will submit to cool argument or logic. It can appear calm and canny or bold and brassy. Highly rated presidential candidates can boastfully challenge pressmen to follow them around, then dissolve their White House hopes with a frivolous fling. Such things defy reason but *define* lust.

Lust involves a dare, a defiance of all strictures, which adds to the final thrill. Sex alone is not enough. In some, lust sees high adventure in walking the edges of deadly disease and disgrace; for others, a more mundane affair is risk enough. But the desirability of *illicit* sex is well demonstrated by the woman who told of her introduction to B&D (bondage and discipline — where tying up and beating one another is part of the sex act): "I was in a frenzy and Tom was thrilled, not having gotten me as excited since our premarital days of heavy petting. Sex once again felt almost taboo."[7]

Another woman, whose husband was addicted to pornography, tried desperately to appease the illicit lust drive by having herself photographed in erotic poses and giving them to her husband for Christmas. She said, "He just put them aside and hasn't looked at them to this day." She was confused and wrote asking "Dear Abby" to shed some light on the situation. Also confused (but not knowing it), Abby suggested methods of finding the source of the man's *low sex drive.*[8]

The Application to Society

Until now we have looked at personal as opposed to cultural seduction. But I am convinced that, while a culture is finally seduced through its individuals, an analogy depicting the culture as an individual can be constructed that will explain the current degradation of America. As a culture, the arts, including TV, might easily be seen as the major senses of sight and hearing. The news media could be compared to the thinking process since the news media forms most of the culture's conclusions.

Probably the most frightening thing about the whole devilish deception of Western civilization is that man prefers deception to truth. John 3:19 clearly informs us that "men love darkness rather than light." Note here that there is no distinction between Christian and non-Christian men. For this reason the war against the flesh is continuous while we live in this world. The church must guard every part of its virtue — always. When some virtue or other is taken for granted, then weakness is revealed and the enemy is able to wear away at the defenses.

As one might suspect, a culture's decision to give in to the societal pimp is a protracted affair. But as surely as a society decides to proceed on a false premise, just so, the repercussions will be equally protracted. The chief difficulty arises from the progressive blindness that occurs, individually or collectively, when a false road is taken. It is very like Bypath

Meadow taken by Bunyan's Pilgrim: it appears to go parallel to the straight and narrow path but it veers slightly. As Richard Weaver has put it,

> [O]ur most serious obstacle is that people traveling this downward path develop an insensitivity which increases with their degradation. . . .
>
> We approach a condition in which we shall be amoral without the capacity to perceive it and degraded without the means to measure our descent.[9]

This peculiar cultural myopia, often called *denial* in the psychological world, not only makes it difficult for us to imagine a world of differing assumptions, but it inculcates a chauvinism of modernism: the automatic rejection of old ideas and standards simply because they are old.

Even Christians fall into the curious trap that old, time-tested prohibitions are *presumed* to be merely *traditions*. This appellation is blithely stamped on these prohibitions without regard for — much less research into — the reasons for their existence. Perhaps we need to learn what the Lord meant in the Old Testament when He warned against moving the ancient landmarks (see, for example, Deuteronomy 19:14 and Proverbs 22:28). Some of the traditions may constitute ancient, spiritual landmarks, and we should move them with some trepidation. Even in my own experience, I have ignored such boundary markers at my own peril — only to discover later why they were originally placed.

Often the seemingly trivial questions of the ancients are key threads in a fabric that, if pulled, threaten to unravel the entire tapestry. On other occasions, the danger comes not from the removal of a thread but the *addition* of a foreign object that cuts or neutralizes the weave.

In some senses, both have happened to Western culture. We now see a ragged, disheveled, immoral America, but the innocuous beginnings were in the Renaissance.

What We Have Seen

- In bait-and-switch it is crucial to capture the attention of the target.

- In prostitution, this is done with *the look.* Proverbs 6:25 confirms this.

- Next, it is necessary to capture the thoughts and imagination (fantasy) of the target. The woman of Proverbs 7 also did this.

- If the target completely rejects the look or the fantasy, the seduction fails. But once the look has led to fantasy and the imaginations have been engaged, the seduction is well under way.

- Seduction leads to a compulsive form of slavery in which the target is led "as an ox" into the skin trade.

- This slavery ends in spiritual and/or physical death. Often it is a protracted and hopeless death.

- When they discover their dying condition, many also find themselves irrevocably trapped in the spiral toward destruction.

- Samson is a good illustration of the entire bait-and-switch sequence, especially when it starts with a seemingly insignificant deviation from God's Word.

- David is an example of a fall during a brief lapse in faithfulness and of an escape from the skin trade after a significant and costly fall. He repented before his sin became habitual. God's grace saved him.

- Solomon demonstrates that God's wisdom without vigilant defense and action will not protect someone from seduction.

- Joseph shows the protective power of long-standing faithfulness to God.

- Satan is the pimp in the skin trade.

- There is reason to believe that important figures in God's work are marked as particular targets for seduction.

- The possibility of losing everything — even though that may be a great deal — appears to be no deterrent to rampant lust.

- The principles of individual seduction (i.e., the look, bait-and-switch, smooth words, fantasy, etc.) may be used for a seduction of a culture or civilization.

- The modern church in the West appears to have neglected these lessons of Scripture.

- One result of this neglect is that Western civilization may be in the terminal stages of the skin trade sequence.

What We Will See

Now we will explore the Love Connection. Toward the end of the Middle Ages, the definition of love changed and was dangled as bait before Western civilization by means of poetry, song, and literature. This laid the foundation for further corruption of Christian principles.

Meanwhile, the church was too caught up in other struggles to regard this shift in the definition of words as important. If it did not lead immediately to sin, it didn't warrant the attention of the church. In reality, this shift was undermining key Scriptural principles on which Christian morality was based. It was only the strength of the existing moral codes that kept behavior in check, but the strength of those codes was eventually eroded as the foundation disappeared.

Another key change was a confusion of idioms between Scripture and the declining culture. The change from the Biblical idiom of the word *heart* — referring to the mind or the soul — to the novel view that the heart was the seat of emotions bolstered the new definition of love. Soon, when these words appeared in Scripture, they were seen with their emotional meanings rather than their proper interpretation.

This seduction into the world of emotion also undermined the authority of God and spiritual guidance in human life, supplanting it with leadership by some notion of "love." The repercussions of this switch are vast.

3

THE LOVE CONNECTION

I t was Ash Wednesday and the sky was overcast. The flagstone courtyard beside the mossy stone church was still damp from the early morning showers. It was a perfect day for the play, *Everyman* — dour and brooding and befitting the beginning of this liturgical season.

Many of the serfs and some independent, itinerant craftsmen were leaving the morning service and gathering at the edges of the plaza, waiting for the play to begin.

A tattered, deep blue curtain had been raised to hide the dressing area and serve as a backdrop. From behind it came the voice of "God" calling to "Death" just as a thick cloud darkened the day further. The whole complement gave out a collective moan — all, that is, except Will, who was stone silent.

Will was a traveling cobbler and was only recently in these parts. He was not much for religion, thinking himself as good as every other man, but he did so enjoy the morality plays.

The people watched as God sent Death to Everyman. Everyman strove fruitlessly to find help—someone to go with him—but in vain. Friends, family, possessions all failed him. Will started as Everyman turned to Good-deeds. She would fain go with him, but alas, she was so weak that she was about to die in the gutter. Everyman's sum of good deeds was a pitiful companion to bring with him to his death.

The comparison was not lost on Will. He reached up under his brown felt cap and scratched his scalp as he pondered the play. *Maybe I'd better prepare for death better,* he thought.

ða   ða   ða

Like the *Everyman* play, much of the early Middle Ages art and literature was devoted to teaching the gospel and the truths of Scripture. However imperfectly done, the accent was on godliness and virtue. But soon the plays, songs, and stories took a decided turn for the worse, and by the late Middle Ages the picture was quite different.

The Middle Ages were in twilight. Many of the gains of the earlier time had been lost to corruption, complacency, and spiritual gangrene. The church had grown corpulent. It ruled, not as a servant in Christ's stead, but as a despot. Many church leaders basked in wealth and cared little for the flock. The noble ruling classes had long neglected their responsibilities to those under them and had become abusive. Serfs were treated as beasts of burden instead of charges of godly care. Luxury and leisure were the lords' goals. They longed to be amused. The mental and spiritual disciplines had grown slack, and nobles pined for their notion of the chivalrous golden age. Of course, the chivalry they imagined and the true ancient chivalry were distinctly different — the true being squarely founded in the Biblical mandates of selfless protection of the weak and the new, idyllic version a figment of a jaded prince's imagination.

Interest in Greek classics and myths abounded as firm reliance on Scripture waned. The whimsy of Greek gods became an entertainment. But it was not entertainment designed to make one ponder. It was amusement, entertainment designed to eliminate thinking. Ruling princes and other nobles, called troubadours, began to entertain themselves with florid songs and yarns about love, heroics, and chivalry — tales of the triumph of "true love."

But true love and chivalry required too much sacrifice, so true love was idealized as a *feeling.* "True love," they sang, "always wins the day." One of the early tales was *Tristan and Iseult* in which the lovers, though unable to overcome the feudal order, were vindicated in death as the two trees growing from their graves intertwined so closely that no one could discern the separation. The switch from love as commitment to love as emotion was made — only in song, mind you.

But this "harmless flirtation" was the amusement they sought. As the origin of the word *amusement* (*a,* without; *muse*, to think deeply or ponder)[1] indicates, these stories actually opposed thought and vaunted feelings — especially romantic feelings.

Yet, at its core, love as an unbridled emotion is as inherently destructive as it is inherently selfish. Love of this sort cares only for how *it* feels and is mortally offended and deeply wounded if the object of its affection does not respond appropriately. Depressions, fits, tantrums, and even murders and suicides often follow unrequited love. Emotions, under control, were regarded in Scripture as having a legitimate place in life, but the new view exalted emotions to a place of control.

It was not that the princes didn't know the truth about love, it was just that their frivolous love songs were so amusing, such *fun*. At first, no one expected anyone to actually believe that love, as a mere emotion, should be the sole motive for marriage or other important decisions.

Many of the noble troubadours hired traveling musicians, called jongleurs, to play and sing the noble compositions at court. Naturally the jongleurs shared these ballads in other courts, or even in the marketplace, for a few coins to ease their wandering way. The minstrel — for entertainment purposes only, you understand — would have introduced the tune with a yarn and a hint that it was all true. Those who saw through the ruse said nothing. After all, it was much more engaging this way; the addition of fantasy enhanced the pleasure.

Rot, Reformation, and Renaissance

During this time of turmoil and decay of institutions, God began to stir things. Fires, lit in the hearts of reformers like John Wycliffe, began to ignite the deep desires of believers to know both God and the Holy Scriptures. But this rekindling was simultaneous with an intellectual rebellion primarily among the nobility, who felt that the solution to church corruption and feudal abuses was to abandon the notion of religious power. This was the distinctly humanist side of the Renaissance. In this move, the contention was made that the church should have no authority over the secular aspects of life. Out of this grew a new sense of nationalism throughout the nations of Europe. Nationalism and intellectualism had previously existed, but all had formerly submitted to the church. With corruption rife in the church of this time, this movement easily gained widespread support.

In addition, the new movable-type printing press spread the word of this Renaissance and gave birth to secular literature. While the new secular literature was flourishing because of the printing press and the love stories were being published in the common languages, the official church violently resisted Bible translations into common speech. In secular literature philosophers and poets began to vaunt the superiority of feeling over fact. But the truth of Scripture was being hamstrung by its alleged chief proponents.

The realists, or classicists, believed that attributes such as love had real existence in their perfected states, and that they were concrete enough to be clearly described. But two other groups of educated men, the nominalists and the conceptualists, challenged this long held belief. The nominalists claimed that these attributes existed merely in name, and conceptualists relegated universals to the realm of human thought. Both saw virtues as philosophical ideals without real substance. This meant that love could not be firmly identified by specific action but could only be tagged by individual feelings. In the old order, God was love, and Scripture clearly delineated what acts or results would follow from a display of God's natures — sin, for instance, could not be motivated by love. But the new thought placed the definition of love in the foggy, ethereal realm of emotion. One might lie, betray, or kill in love's service.

The struggle between these two schools of thought went on for centuries. The medieval scholars labored under the handicap of untranslated Bibles but still produced reams of defense for godly virtue. The nominalists and the conceptualists did not so much answer these scholars, as they put their own philosophy to work as entertainment: song, theater, and books. None of the new thinkers who valued their heads would directly deny God. They simply separated the virtuous attributes from God and idealized them.

Formerly, stories afforded only faint indications of the feelings of the characters. The focus of the story was an appealing exaltation of virtue — virtues which were regarded as attainable graces from God. *The Song of Roland* is typical of this kind of literature, and the Bible is similarly written (to the great dismay of the modern psychologized religionists). In fact, this peculiar lack of emotional description in Scripture is positively stunning. Scripture did not *deny* or *decry* emotion, but recognized it as *subservient* to spirit and intellect. Emotional devices were not unknown in literature during the time when the Biblical books were penned. Greek lyrics had epitomized the genre and provided a model for the troubadours and jongleurs. Even the most florid of Biblical writings, The Song of Solomon, shows a singularly intelligent and committed love.[2] Surely, when the Song says that "love is strong as death" (8:6), it is not referring to emotional love, which is often defeated by mood, weather, time of day, exhaustion, and a host of other incidentals. Entirely lacking in the Song is the "your-love-makes-*me*-feel" self-centeredness of most love songs.

But it is not so much that the inclusion of emotion was wrong, it was that the virtues were no longer regarded as real and definable. They had become mere ideals to be sought and *felt*. In *Roland,* the virtue of courage, for instance, existed regardless of his feelings. In later works, it became necessary for the hero to *feel* courage well up in his heart. The impact on the reader was emotional. Rather than a stimulus to courage, it was an invitation to *feel* courageous.

The shift was subtle, beginning with gushing trib-
utes like Chrétien de Troyes' *Lancelot* and moving toward utterly pragmatic works like Machiavelli's political handbook, *The Prince*. It grew over the years to the
point where the romantic ideals of the nominalists
were even spoofed by their own in the seventeenth-
century work, *Don Quixote*. Yet Cervantes' *Don Quixote* ended on the curious note that even idealistic delusions may serve an important purpose: man *needs* to
tilt at windmills, to *feel* the call to action. No matter
that the feeling led one to foolishness. The other pole
ranged from the morality tales, *Everyman* and Dante's
Inferno, to useful studies such as Thomas 'a Kempis's
Imitation of Christ.

In the epic poem *The Song of Roland,* the hero is
shown to be courageous and sacrificial — but also
proud and stubborn. These attributes are clearly displayed without comment regarding their origin or the
feelings of the character. It was as if to say that
Roland's *feelings* would not justify his pride, nor
would they diminish his courage. Conversely, the adulterous woman in the thirteenth-century French tale,
Chasteline De Vergi, who dies from grief over her inordinate affair being exposed, seems to be vindicated
by her feelings of love. In spite of the heroine's death,
this theme of outwitting a jealous husband became a
standard device in lighter verse and common literature.

So the division between secular and sacred became
ever more stark. Once the separation had been made
between spiritual and secular, people began to imagine

that, while God might reign in one arena, man was certainly master of the other. The humanist mentality was forming.

In this atmosphere, classical Greek heroism, combined with the chivalric ballads of the troubadours, grew in popularity. Because of the printing press, such tales were more durable and widely broadcast. Another distinct advantage of the romantic literature was that it was in the common language. In fact, romanticism comes from the word *romanz* which means "the language of the people." Being in print also lent enormous additional credibility to the stories. But contrary to Biblical stories and the morality plays displayed in earlier times, these Greek-inspired, idealized tales were not founded on solid, moral principles. All the while, the European mind was slowly being poisoned by a redefinition of *love*. They had taken their first glance — they had caught *the look* — and were being drawn to the bait. The romance was on!

Meanwhile, the church was embattled with serious doctrinal and moral crises and devoted little effort to such seemingly trivial matters as the definition of *love*. Eventually, though, these small beginnings developed into the movement called romanticism.

Romanticism's Ruse

Romeo: O, wilt thou leave me so unsatisfied?

Juliet:	What satisfaction canst thou have to-night?
Romeo:	Th' exchange of thy love's faithful vow for mine.
Juliet:	I gave thee mine before thou didst request it; And yet I would it were to give again.
Romeo:	Wouldst thou withdraw it? For what purpose, love?
Juliet:	But to be frank, and give it thee again. And yet I wish but for the thing I have. My bounty is as boundless as the sea, My love as deep: the more I give to thee, The more I have, for both are infinite.[3]

This famous scene from Shakespeare's *Romeo and Juliet* perhaps epitomizes the romantic literature of the time. Here are two teenagers who have met only that same day at the equivalent of a high school dance, and already they are exchanging eternal vows of love "boundless as the sea" and "infinite." Centuries later, the urgency of Romeo's "Wilt thou leave me unsatisfied?" would be more crudely and more urgently repeated by Elvis Presley singing, "It's now or never; my love won't wait. Kiss me my darlin'; be mine tonight."[4]

The whole play could have been done in blue jeans — and in fact, was, under the title of *West Side Story*. Of course, there will be some who argue the difference in the literary value of the two, but the essential point in these examples is that they were all, like advertising, designed for mass appeal. They were written in the language of the people, the *romanz* for their time.

Romanticism, however, was more than just literature in the common tongue. It was an entire philosophy predicated on the victory of feeling over fact, the notion that man's innate emotions could be trusted as a guide. Romanticism should not be confused with the connotations associated with the word *romance,* but was a glorifying of certain emotional ideals such as love, courage, and loyalty. It was not the actual traits of love, courage, and loyalty that romantic literature lionized, but the feelings of those things; its intent was not to promote real love, courage, or loyalty but to evoke the feelings of those traits. Romanticism reacted to the realism and rationalism of earlier times by emphasizing the individual rather than others, the subjective rather than the verifiable, and the spontaneous over the formal. It exalted the beauties of nature and the senses over the intellect.

While the troubadours touted emotional love as the ultimate ideal, it was the literature of romanticism that indicated that it was a universally attainable ideal. "Love," it was saying, "is what fulfills everyone. It is everyone's birthright." More and more the stories began to use the *feeling* of love, or another of the romantic ideals, to justify immoral acts.

Such notables as Shakespeare held love aloft as the glittering ideal, the solution of problems, and the crux of all true tragedy. By this time, books were in abundance, and even common people were beginning to learn the art of reading.

With the reduction of church power and its corresponding loss of importance in people's lives, people were spiritually defenseless when the bait of romance was dangled enticingly before their eyes. Anecdotes of love's triumph over insurmountable difficulties seemed to prove love's all-encompassing power and everyone's need for love. There was a division in their minds over the meaning of the word as used in the church and as it was used in the "real world." Of course, the "real world" was where these people lived most of their lives. It was, by this time, difficult to turn their affections from this newfound love. Little did they realize that the love they would eventually get was not the love that was being advertised in literature. But they had already taken the bait.

Yet the new definition of love posed a dilemma: Given the moral framework that still existed regarding sexual matters, how was the love in these stories to resolve itself? Certainly the lovers could not simply gaze into each other's eyes forever; nor could they consummate their love without marriage. Of course, they were married in the end, their love overcoming all obstacles, and "they lived happily ever after." Even in the tragedies where the lovers died, love was touted as the strongest force. The moral endings, however, were only necessary in the more publicly acceptable literature. Many of the street-level songs, poetry, and stories, like Chaucer's *The Miller's Tale,* carried the ribald theme of outwitting the jealous husband. Naturally, the husbands of these tales were petty, boorish tyrants who deserved the unfaithfulness of their wives. The ill feelings toward the husband served to seal the justification of the woman's adultery. In effect, the moral force of virtue lost out to the more sensually potent, amoral force of feeling.

But the real attack here was against the underlying assumption that marriage was an institution designed *primarily* for and by God rather than to fulfill the desires and emotional needs of men and women. The purpose of Christian marriage had formerly been viewed as (1) glorifying God, (2) raising godly children, (3) serving as a model of the unity of Christ and the church, (4) a stabilizing influence on the larger family and society, and (5) an opportunity to give to another in a selfless manner. Into this chain was injected the concept of fulfilling powerful (though not necessarily mutual) emotional needs.

Literature portrayed this emotional experience as primary. And while all the other purposes were true, it implied, "love" must be present for marriage to succeed. Since it required a priest to be married, the clergy in romantic literature, like Friar Lawrence in *Romeo and Juliet,* were often co-conspirators with the lovers to help them bring their love to a "proper" conclusion. Marriage began to be viewed as a consummation of an emotional state rather than a commitment of love in the Biblical sense. This had deep consequences for the stability of marriage as young ladies began to balk at well-arranged marriages because of romantic dreams of thrilling emotions. Dissatisfied women strained their marriages because of the missing romance. Men sought adventures of love in images and imaginations of erotica.

The Sanctification of Love

A second effect of the elevation of love to near-divine status was the inversion of man's hierarchy of command. Early church thinkers, using Scripture, envisioned man as body, soul, and spirit. In this seemingly simple formula, they said, was a proper chain of command for man. Permeating the entire triad was the fallenness of human nature. While there were certain disagreements about the exact boundaries of the human triptych, there was genuine and general agreement as to the order and preeminence.

It was assumed that all people would submit first to God—the ultimate authority. To this realm belonged God Himself, the Scriptures, and, to a lesser extent, established doctrines and traditions. Man's spirit was seen as the point of contact between man and the spirit world. Spiritual activity outside of submission to God resulted, they said, in unfounded mysticism and unbridled witchcraft. Man's spirit was designed to bow to and communicate with God alone.

From this submissive position, the human spirit was to guide the soul using the innate conscience and divine revelation. The soul was considered the seat of the intellect, the will, the intentions — in essence, the mind. The soul, under authority of the spirit, was to control the body. But a man who was ruled by his soul without the line of authority through God and his own spirit would be willful, utterly pragmatic, calculating, and devoid of the constraints of morality or compassion.

The body, on the other hand, was viewed as much more than an animated corpse. It included the senses and even the emotions. Since emotions were primarily sensations, they were classed with the body under the lump term, the *flesh*. As such, it was often viewed with suspicion simply because it was the weakest link of the tripartite nature of man. People were often tempted to act upon their emotions or other sensations without mitigation from the spirit and the soul. A man ruled by his body was sensual and completely bestial.

But the redefinition of *love* sabotaged this entire understanding of man's nature. When the status of love was elevated to the spiritual level, it upended the hierarchy of authority and placed sensation in the driver's seat. Love was then viewed as a "good" emotion. And more, it was regarded as particularly Christian — especially when Scripture announces, "God is love," like a stamp of approval. The effects of such confusion were profound, even though the changes occurred slowly due to societal restraints imposed by Christianity.

The "Heart" in Heat

The church seemed prepared to accommodate the substitution of language so long as it did not result in overt sexual sin. This shallow view was a serious blunder because not only did it undermine the sanctity of marriage, it would eventually destroy the sanctity of life itself. Part of the church's accommodation to this deception was a failure to protect another term from distortion — the *heart*.

In scriptural idiom, the heart is synonymous with the mind or the soul, hence the reference to "the thoughts and intents of the heart" (Hebrews 4:12). But romantic literature equated the heart with the emotions — particularly the "soft" emotions. People who did not respond emotionally were denigrated as cold- or hard-hearted. This change also helped validate emotion as a ruling element in people's lives. Every Scripture referring to the heart was seen as tacit support for this notion. For instance, when Scripture commands Christians to "forgive from the heart" (see Matthew 18:35) those who had offended them, believers imagined they were obligated to *feel* forgiveness for the transgressor.

This demonic substitution was addressed by C. S. Lewis in his insightful *Screwtape Letters* where the elder devil advises the younger:

> Keep them watching their own minds and trying to produce *feelings* there by the action of their own wills. When they meant to ask Him for charity, let

them, instead, start trying to manufacture charitable *feelings* for themselves and not notice that this is what they are doing. When they meant to pray for courage, let them really be trying to *feel* brave. When they say they are praying for forgiveness, let them be trying to *feel* forgiven. Teach them to estimate the value of each prayer by their success in producing the desired *feeling*.[5] (Emphasis added.)

In this, the true focus of forgiveness is lost. When it comes to the forgiveness of others, the decision and commitment to forgive — to hold nothing against another — is swallowed up in the shallow attempt to *feel* something good for the offending party. Once again, there is the triumph of feeling over fact. In this case, one may avoid *doing* what Christ commands as long as a proper feeling can be produced.

Despite the efforts of scriptural reformers, it seemed that most Europeans were adopting the new definitions. The hidden hook was the philosophy which elevated man's emotions over God's Word. All of this was part of Satan's hidden agenda to enslave and prostitute civilization. The bait was "love" from the "heart" and Western man bit. What he *really* got was slavery. Western civilization was being led to the auction block of the skin trade.

What We Have Seen

- Toward the end of the Middle Ages, the church was corrupt and the princes had become lax and abusive.

- A growing interest in ungodly pagan myths and a yearning for a "golden age" of chivalry led troubadours to compose songs and tales of bravery, battle, and the power of "love" to overcome obstacles.

- Simultaneously, God raised up men such as John Wycliffe to reintroduce the Scriptures as a curative to the corruption of the time.

- The official church was too embroiled in its own political conflict to see the idle, pagan-inspired works as a significant problem.

- The invention of the movable-type printing press flooded Europe with copies of these tales in ordinary speech while the official church violently hindered the printing of Bibles in the languages of the people.

- Eventually, the love stories became the wellspring of what became known as romantic literature.

- Love was presented as a feeling that sometimes justified some kinds of immoral behavior, though, generally, sexual morals were upheld.

- The newly defined *love* undermined the Christian view of the purposes of marriage.

- The word *heart* became an idiom for emotion rather than mind.

- These new definitions of *love* and *heart* challenged the spiritual and natural hierarchy of authority within man and placed emotions in control of acts.

- The deadly duo of destructive definitions carried over into the reading of Scripture, and many people began to interpret key verses from an emotional base.

• It soon became plausible for people to boldly disobey the Word of God and still imagine themselves justified because they had evoked the proper *feelings.*

What We Will See

The consequences of these seemingly insignificant ideas were minute at first but they quickly broadened. But there was a new dimension of deception waiting in the wings. Secularism was preparing to introduce a new understanding of the universe — naturalism. This "science" propounded a world in which the natural order was an ultimate truth.

Prior to this time, the universe was viewed as a fallen creation, but one in which the glory of God was still, though imperfectly, reflected. Naturalism saw the creation as complete — nearly deified — and a reflection of how things should be. Right and wrong, it taught, could be discerned by what was natural.

This was a dispassionate form of nature worship. The conclusions of naturalism laid the foundations for the later acceptance of premarital sex and hedonism.

4

MR. NATURAL
AND THE SEXUAL
REVOLUTION

I t's pure and natural," bleats the ad. While milk is
being poured over a hearty breakfast cereal, visions
of countrysides filled with flowing wheat stalks, robust
farmers, clear, sunny skies, and a sparkling, trout-filled
stream immediately come to mind. One could hardly
think of a higher recommendation than being *natural.*
This blurb sells everything from bath soap to bottled
water, from hair coloring to hedonism.

Hedonism? you wonder.

Yes, hedonism.

It wasn't long after the widespread acceptance of
the Love Myth that the new thinkers realized that emotions formed a very flimsy base upon which to con-
struct real life. What worked out perfectly well in plays
and lyric poems didn't seem to provide substantial

footing for daily existence. Still, they were loathe to admit that the old scholars might have been right after all with their established morals and fixed virtues.

They felt that something more rational was needed for the business of living. This was not rationalism as the old realists had it with its utter dependence on absolutes from God and Scripture, but a human rationalism.

The first neorationalism wound up in the cultural garbage heap because it was purely intellectual and emotionally sterile — emotions that the great majority had already come to accept as essential to life. Cold rationalism iced the progress of humanism. When the enthronement of Reason[1] in post-revolution France revealed itself as the Reign of Terror and drenched the godless nation with blood, it was obvious that reason alone was insufficient.[2] It was important that humanist philosophers discover some means of appearing rational while allowing the emotions free reign.

So, out of the dustbin they pulled the ancient Greek idea of *natural law*. But natural law was a precept often used by the church. Even Jesus used a certain level of nature in parables to define the kingdom of God. The naturalists were treading dangerous ground. Using natural law posed the same problem as allowing God into the picture when defining *love*. Up until now, nature had been viewed as an imperfect, or fallen, reflection of God's glory. While some analogies from nature could be drawn, it was undependable as an authoritative source of God's wisdom. But the naturalists hid under the guise of science and announced their startling discovery: Nature is natural!

Natural Art

Naturalist thinking left its mark on the arts. Paintings and literature displayed a "slice of life" but suspended moral judgment. The heavy humanism of the Renaissance drew art from its mission to teach and spiritually elevate and focused on humanity. Portrait painting became an artistic staple. Naturalism even exalted the backgrounds of the portraits. Where in the past most nature scenes were mere coronas around human subjects, the nature scenes gradually became the subjects. Soon the subjects were a combination of persons and natural scenes — as if to say that it was all one big, happy, natural, organic picnic. Often vices, especially sexual vices, were part of the "natural" scene. But, again, morality had no place. Artists who remained in the realist school, which attempted to attract the viewer to virtue or repel him from vice, were systematically excluded because they insisted on moral judgment as a component of their work.

As with the earlier romanticism, it was again art and literature that carried the message. Western man, now extremely sense-oriented, was shown the pastoral scenes of debauchery in the woods, and it *felt* right. Further, when artists rendered Darwin's evolutionary ascent, it was perfectly natural for people to accept the

superficial similarities of man and ape as positive proof
of the hypothesis. With Darwin's hypothesis, humanists were at last free from that final restraint — God.
God had become a vestigial appendage — and He was
the final reason for *any* moral standards.

A Science Is Born

The new naturalism defined all beings and events as
natural. The supernatural was either denied outright or
reduced to being unknown natural phenomena. Science
took much the same tack by declaring all nature to be
knowable. Things that were not knowable simply did
not exist. The seventeenth-century philosopher, Baruch
Spinoza exemplified this belief saying, "Nature always
observes laws and rules . . . although they may not all
be known to us, and therefore she keeps a fixed and
immutable order. . . . What is meant in Scripture by a
miracle can only be a work of Nature."[3]
Such thinking became very popular among the
church "intellectualoids."[4] They posited that God,
good, and evil could be known by either nature or revelation, but the secret was that nature was actually *superior.* There was an embarrassed silence among
churchmen when some bumpkin of a preacher propounded orthodox beliefs. It became fashionable by the
nineteenth century to actively seek naturalistic explanations for the miracles of the Bible. Darwin's discoveries sealed the fate of the old believers in the supernatu-

ral. Christians, thinking themselves outgunned, re-treated to a last ditch defense of the existence of God and the fallen nature of man. Both of these, the naturalists granted them — for the time being.

Freud and the Demise of Morality

Then Sigmund Freud began dismantling the fallen nature of man by presenting man as a mechanistic, materialistic bundle of experiences and responses.[5] Guilt and sin were useless, even harmful concepts. Civilization had abandoned reason guided by Scripture, and the basis for even simple morality was undercut. Only unfounded consensus determined morality and, if anyone had cared to look, there was no foundation beneath even that. Freud's work spawned many followers, but they usually fell into one of two camps: (1) live with your guilt, or (2) blame it on somebody else. Neither had any fixed point of right and wrong. Freud added that even man's evil doings were not evil, but natural, considering the traumas of childhood and the conflict of the id and superego.

Overwhelmed Christian die-hards cried, "Foul!" But their voices were slowly squeezed out as more and more of the "enlightened" took up ranks in the church's leadership and seminaries.[6]

Right and wrong were passé. Morality, the naturalist said, was not knowable. Natural things, he said, were not subject to moral scrutiny. After all, what moral judgment could be brought against a wolf that killed a peasant's sheep; it was only doing what its nature demanded. Nature was natural, the naturalists said, and what was natural was good.

Opposing Definitions of *Natural*

This was a boon to the rising humanist movement because man was natural. The goodness of man was a "natural" conclusion. Naturalism, in unholy alliance with the Love Myth, created the illusion that raw emotion was also natural and thus, good. It was easy for them to believe and teach that man's deepest emotions would always lead him right. In fact, the *presumption* of humanism is that man's inner self is always right.

The Scriptures, on the other hand, presented another meaning for *natural*. The natural man was regarded as the corrupt seed of Adam, the carnal nature, and the stain of original sin. Even nature itself bore witness to the ultimate untrustworthiness of the natural state. After all, weren't weeds easier to grow than fruit or flowers? And weren't the superior fruits and flowers the cultivated ones?[7] The very thing that was held aloft by naturalists as the hope of man was the thing that was the reason for man's corruption.

But such arguments were lost on the now sensual population. The appeal of nature *felt* so much more compelling. The fallen beauty of the earth, as idealized in paintings and literature, may have been in stark contrast to the daily mud and blood of life for most people, but Western man was already sold on good feelings. He now blindly followed the false rationalism and the feelings that he was convinced would not lead him wrong.

The Compromise of the Church

The retreating church had already capitulated to science on other issues and submitted Scripture to scientific proof instead of the other way around. The "irrational" insistence of some Christians on full Biblical authority made them the recipients of ridicule even within church ranks. Slowly, the church's base was eroded until, in the twentieth century, there was open, unconditional surrender. Much of the church agreed to submit publicly and politically to the dictates of science as long as it was allowed to cling to the remnants of God-belief on Sundays.

The once-powerful body of Christ was covered with wounds — self-inflicted reminders of its pitiful compromise. Christians committed to combating the sensual, naturalistic takeover of Western civilization were profoundly weakened as church leaders remained silent or defected.

Love and naturalism's strange progeny continued to multiply, and evil effects began to appear. Some people began to realize the switch (from the bait-and-switch) and loudly denounce it, but the culture was committed to its headlong pursuit of pleasure.

Selling Sex to the People

Emotions were soon included under the cover of "natural." A view emerged that man was like a bag which contained emotions. Suppression of emotions was posited as dangerous since the bag might overfill and burst and uncontrollably scatter its contents. Or perhaps a leak would develop and the person would engage in some perversion. Freud thought that all perversions came from bottled-up raw emotions. He encouraged the venting of emotions to prevent such distortion.[8]

Of course, sex was a logical way to vent the emotion of love. And, lo and behold, it was discovered: *sex is natural!* Not only was venting love good for the psyche, but as a cure it was also good and natural. So natural, in fact, that there was soon common traffic in using the word *love* for sex.

This linkage was deadly. In the popular mind, love became an emotion whose natural fulfillment was in sex. The cultural pimp was crouching at the door, waiting to sell the West into "the action" and to get people to act on the new assumptions.

The advance men for this phase—the selling of people into sex—were highly visible people such as Walt Whitman, Havelock Ellis, and Margaret Sanger. All of them argued the naturalness of sex as though its very naturalness meant there should be no restriction. Ellis even included some perversion in his argument.[9] Whitman brushed against homosexuality.[10] Sanger insisted feverishly that liberated sex would usher in a golden age of peace and prosperity. In fact, she saw inhibitions about sex as the single greatest problem facing mankind.

> The great central problem, and the one which must be taken first is the abolition of the shame and fear of sex. We must teach men the overwhelming power of this radiant force. . . . Through sex, mankind may attain the great spiritual illumination which will transform the world, which will light up the only path to an earthly paradise.[11]

Sanger was a woman with a mission, and she worked tirelessly to spread her "spiritual illumination" to everyone.

Most of society was not quite ready for such views — or their corresponding activities — but was strangely drawn by the internally consistent logic. Having abandoned an authoritative Bible and a holy God, they found themselves without much of a debate platform. It was only the prevailing sexual mores — changeable as they were — that briefly slowed the slide into the sexual slime.

Nails in the Coffin

Skinny Margaret, white and soft, squatted with the young, black-skinned girls of the village outside the hut. Margaret Mead was twenty-three but the girls were in their teens. They all laughed and giggled.

The balmy, cloudless day lent itself to their state of minimum dress. The girls were telling Margaret of their sexual adventures—how they flitted like butter-flies from one man to another. "Was this not natural?" they seemed to ask.

Margaret was thrilled. She had long believed in the *noble savage*—that man in his natural state was more upright than so-called civilized man. She had instinct-ively known that lowered restrictions in sex led to a healthier society. She had found no rape here, no mur-ders in jealous rages. In fact, all crime was low. The women were not oppressed or thought of as chattel. The girls' stories confirmed their ease with the sub-ject—not to mention the activities—of sex. Here was the noble savage played out in everyday life. This would finally put the old moralists in their place.

After only five months with the Samoans, she wrote *Coming of Age in Samoa,* about the free-wheel-ing sexual practices of these people. The study was an instant hit, especially in the sexually liberated crowd of the Roaring Twenties. It became—and remains—one of the cornerstones of modern anthropological educa-tion.

There was only one problem—the girls lied.[12]

                      ❧   ❧   ❧

Ever since the Enlightenment, there had been a growing myth of the *noble savage*. This proposal stated that mankind was basically good and that, re-moved from the artificial strictures of religion and civi-lization, the goodness would naturally surface. There was a growing body of literature that carried this theme. James Fenimore Cooper and Edgar Rice Burroughs were strong proponents of the idea.[13] Reports of cultures in the South Seas and the Orient seemed to corroborate the belief. Some rumors were of paradisal, tropical lands where there was no war, no crime — just natural man living in harmony with his environment and his neighbor.

It was just such tales that compelled the youthful Margaret Mead to so blindly seek proof of the noble savage. From her studies, she concluded that restrictions of natural drives caused crime in civilization. Rules, laws, norms, and moral codes, she asserted like a good naturalist, created a tension that increased crime.

The world was ready to hear that message. The naturalistic, evolutionist world of science gobbled it up and blindly groped for similar evidence elsewhere. Suddenly, "stone age" tribes were popping up like weeds. *All* were peace-loving, nonviolent, and sexually liberated (and after the feminist movement began, nonsexist, i.e., sharing housework and child rearing). These were unspoiled by interference from civilization, alias Christianity. It hardly seemed to matter that, in some cases, these "tribesmen" had been seen months earlier in a village wearing bell-bottom pants and T-shirts[14] The noble savage must survive. No one mentioned that the truly primitive tribes had ritualized human sacrifice, cannibalism, and, sometimes, incest. Despite thorough debunking, Margaret Mead and her

Samoan hoax are still received as *de rigueur* in anthropological circles.

The natural man lives on — that is, the natural man of Scripture, the one that loves darkness rather than light.

What We Have Seen

- After the Love Myth had gotten a firm hold on the imagination of the West, naturalism made its debut.

- Naturalism taught that all things were natural and that nothing truly supernatural existed. Nature, it taught, was the highest court of appeal and what was natural was right.

- The church was weakened in its fight against naturalism because it had already assented to the superiority of science over Biblical revelation in a number of areas.

- The hypotheses of Darwin and Freud created an apparently final blow to the Christian position and entrenched the teachings of naturalism.

- All things natural came to be regarded as good.

- Emotions, and especially love, came to be included under the heading of natural (and thus, good).

- Sex was viewed as natural and the natural fulfillment of emotional love.

- In the late nineteenth and early twentieth centuries, promoters of sexual liberation began to get a hearing in public forums. Walt Whitman, Havelock Ellis, and Margaret Sanger were among the proponents.

- While much of society objected to their outright conclusions, society was sufficiently drugged by their false beliefs on love and sex that little ground was found to oppose them.

- Science soon began to fabricate evidence of the natural goodness of man and sex.

What We Will See

Western civilization has been seduced — fallen for the bait-and-switch. What has been the result? How has that seduction enslaved mankind in the skin trade? Each of the next few chapters will sum up a different aspect of the skin trade's hold on the West: pornography, prostitution, homosexuality, and the free-sex culture.

The next chapter reveals how a new form of "literature" developed from the worst aspects of the Love Myth and naturalism. This is the introduction of what is recognized today as pornography. This creeping smut grew from a wealthy collector's obsession to the $8-billion-a-year industry it is today. It predictably led from a few etchings of nude women to the bestial and obscene depictions in the adult bookstores.

What effect does this gross distortion of the gift of sex have on individuals? on families? on communities? on culture?

5

PORNO PITFALL

J erry Butler, a striking blonde star of over four hundred porno movies, was explaining to Margie, the
radio show hostess, about the mistreatment of the talent in the porno industry. He spoke of a recent film
where the actors never received their pay.

"Wait a minute," said the hostess. "You end your
[book] by saying you're getting out of the business.
Does this mean you've changed your mind — you're
back in?"

Butler stammers, "Well . . . I have to ad-
mit . . . yes, I did . . . I did a couple of productions.
That was about two weeks ago. I'd be lying to you if I
didn't . . . "

"Is it an addiction?" Margie pressed.

"Yes, it is. It is an addiction. It's something that
I've done so many times — over and over again."

"And you feel like you can't stop?"

Again he stammers, almost apologetically, "I'm trying . . . the best that I could . . . I've done a lot less than I've ever done before."

Margie continues to probe, asking about his wife and child. He is opposed to government controls against porn, but he admits that he does not want his child to be exposed to pornography. He claims his wife supports his attempts to leave the business even though he often fails.

"Jerry," Margie asks sympathetically, "you sound mixed up to me. You sound like you want to quit, but then you don't quit . . . "

"Isn't that what an addict is all about?" he blurts. "Somebody who is pretty much confused because of the passion and the romance that he has with the business. . . . I will always be a porno actor—no matter even if I'm out for five years."[1]

ა.   ა.   ა.

"Pornography is all in your mind," they tell me—*they* being the proponents of obscenity. And I find myself in agreement, for the sustenance of porn is fantasy. In truth, fantasy plays a major role in *all* illicit sex. Look how the adulteress in Proverbs 7 paints a seductive mental picture of her boudoir and the "loves" within. Jesus gave importance to this truth when He announced that it was adultery to simply look and lust after a woman (see Matthew 5:28). Certainly no one commits adultery without going through this fantasy stage, but in pornography the fantasy is the *entire* thing.

But the cruel bondage of fantasy is a stronger fetter than could be forged by any human slaver. Here, the impulses of one's own body exalt themselves over the spirit and the soul and contemptuously overrun the conscience. The stories I've heard from many porn addicts is *prima facea* evidence of this. The above story of Jerry Butler illustrates the hold that "the romance" of porn has on people.

In the Beginning

Pornography began as sexually explicit tales told or written to stimulate the sexual drives of men. As far back as ancient Greece, pornography (*porneo graphos* — the writings of prostitutes) has been found in this form. While there was some Greek art devoted to this genre, most of the nude statuary was distinctly nonsexual. Through the ages, the pornographic writings were restricted to wealthy collectors, but tales and songs could be presented to anyone who happened to be at the tavern when the wandering minstrel appeared. And as long as sexual sins could be confined to the occasional work of imaginations, it was not so likely to become obsessive. Few could find sufficient free time to seek constant arousal.

Once again the printing press played a major role. While such printings were surreptitious, there was a growing market for it. There was no law which regulated the smut, save the law of shame — a man would have been shamed to have it publicly known that he trafficked in such swill. Not until the case of Sir Charles Sedley in 1663 did public obscenity became a legal issue.[2] He had stood drunk and naked on a balcony in the middle of London shouting obscenities at pedestrians and dousing passersby with urine. This case decided that obscenity constituted a public damage of morals.

During the eighteenth century, a U.S. postal inspector named Anthony Comstock watched with growing dismay as the U.S. mail was used to transmit lurid literature to people all over the country. He was appalled that a government service was the vehicle of vice and set about to change that. His active crusade brought about the enactment and enforcement of federal laws.

Proliferation through Photography

At this time, printing was becoming cheaper. Etchings of naked women became the stock-in-trade of the panderer. By the turn of the century, photography came of age, and mass printing of "dirty French postcards" and other underground pressruns surfaced in the seedier edges of society. General public disgust at these productions was prevalent. Though many of the proponents claimed to be "admiring the natural beauty of the human form," those of "common morality" laughed at such misdirection. But underneath the laughter was a hollow place where the rational justification for morality used to dwell. So while moralists struggled to stem the spread of immorality, their own false presuppositions about the nature of love and sex undercut their efforts. The sensualism and naturalism accepted by Western civilization in the arena of science was flatly rejected in arguments on morals and ethics. Many free sex proponents saw the flagrant gap and rightly branded it hypocrisy.

Already there was cultural acceptance of nudity and sexuality (though mostly somewhat demure references) as art. It wasn't long before the societal pimps included the "art" argument in their arsenal. The opposition was fading fast. Nobody, it seemed, wanted to be seen as opposed to art. This also reflected the feelings of those who waged moral warfare in the intellectual fields — the feeling that those who opposed the naturalistic view were anti-intellectual.

The first to take full advantage of the "sophistication" technique to sell pornography was Hugh Hefner in the 1950s. Seemingly a far cry from both the raunchy underground magazines and the more timid men's magazines like *Esquire,* Hefner's *Playboy* actually combined elements of both. Hefner transferred the high production values of *Esquire* on to the gritty images of nude women. He kept the sophisticated, philosophical tone but included the overt nudity and sexuality that *Esquire* was loathe to do.

The image of the pipe-smoking intellectual wearing a silk cravat was projected in the place of the seedy degenerate, but the cleanup and clothing change did not alter the underlying perversion. The image, however, was all part of the fantasy.[3] It wasn't long before child sex, bestiality, incest, drug use, and violent sex were tacitly or overtly condoned as part of the lifestyle of untrammeled freedom. But this freedom was soon to enslave millions.

A Picture's Worth

I only saw it out of the corner of my eye, but I froze in my tracks. I was only about seven years old, and I was hurrying through the cluttered drugstore to the candy section clutching my allowance when I saw it.

The paperback rack stood like Goliath just beside the candy shelves. On it was a book whose darkly painted cover displayed a naked woman tied to a tree. Of course, other things in the picture seemed to barely cover her in certain places.

I had no idea what those "places" would look like — or why they should be covered. But I *knew* they should be covered.

I tried to avert my eyes. I knew I shouldn't look. I was sure the drugstore man would see me look and . . . and . . . and I didn't know what would happen then. I spent what seemed to be hours selecting my candy, all the while sneaking surreptitious glances at the forbidden sight. When I left, I felt soiled, sweaty, ashamed, but secretly thrilled in a way I didn't understand.

I found many reasons to return to the drugstore over the next few weeks and visit the dark, enigmatic vision. Each time the shame was further submerged and the unnamed excitement grew. My sexual fantasy life had begun — and I didn't even know it.

    🙢   🙢   🙢

Because photographic images required less work of the imagination than written or spoken pornography, photography spurred pornography to new heights. The super-fast presses of the mid-twentieth century made cheap pornography available everywhere. Increased leisure time allowed men to attempt to satiate this bottomless desire. The easy visions also stirred more powerful drives toward sex, especially among the young. Coupled with masturbation, pornography linked sexual satisfaction with obsession. This obsession enslaved the young men brought into its sphere of influence and drove them to seek more and more explicit material.

An immensely powerful chain reaction was started. Idle curiosity became an addiction which linked man's most potent pleasure with sexual pictures. But, like all addictions, there was an increase in the substance needed to generate the desired pleasure. More deviant material was demanded to boost the waning thrills of "soft-core" pornography. *Playboy* tried to keep up with the escalation by gingerly approaching taboo subjects through its letters column or through humor.[4]

This encroachment on the forbidden usually triggers some response from the conscience. Man's psyche then responds with the characteristic self-justification of fallen human nature by convincing itself that such bizarre sexual practices are normal. Once this self-deceit is thoroughly accomplished, man soon feels compelled to act upon his newfound freedom by insisting that wives, girlfriends, prostitutes, or even strangers perform the acts seen in the pornography.[5] Some of this compulsion may be a further attempt at self-justification, but in any case, the effects can be catastrophic.

During the early years of the porn explosion, the schizophrenic culture in America struggled to be liberated from the old morality and to define pornography for the purposes of legal prosecution. Gone were the days of a U.S. Supreme Court justice who crowed that he could not define pornography, but he knew it when he saw it. Firmer definition than community standards alone was needed. Where shame and social rejection could have — and should have — provided a plumbline, an uncertain populace looked to the courts. The *Roth v. United States*[6] decision by the U.S. Supreme Court, which presumed that whatever was obscene was *automatically* lacking in social value, decreed that material that appealed to the prurient interest in sex was obscene.

It seemed like a victory for morality. But *Roth* represented an obvious loss of a consensus of moral behavior. Worse still, the approval of obscenity prosecution by the high court brought no response from the legal community.[7] Facing continuous (and expensive) challenges from the ACLU and its ilk, prosecutions continued to drop for the next two decades as obscenity became a low-priority crime. Meanwhile, rape and molestation were skyrocketing.

The Bondage of Culture

The phone gave a sudden ring. I reached around from my worktable, nearly knocking over one of the precariously perched piles of papers and snatched the receiver.

"'ello," I said, cinching the phone between chin and shoulder.

"Mr. Dupree?" came the woman's voice.

"That's me," I answered, ignoring the mispronounced name.

"Were you on TV . . . I think I saw you on TV a couple of months back talking about pornography. Was that you?"

"Probably was," I answered, sensing some urgency in her voice. "How can I help you?"

"Well," she said haltingly — not ready for such a direct question. "Well, I just want to say I agree with what you said about porn — it being addicting and all." After some verbal meandering, she finally said, "What can I do? My husband . . . "

The tragedy unfolded. She had been married years ago to a man who liked pornography. But it soon grew out of control. He began to pressure her into strange sex. When she refused, he hit her. He ran around with other women and finally molested some children.

He was in prison now, and she had long since divorced him.

She knew her new husband liked an occasional *Playboy,* but now she had discovered a cache of harder stuff. She confronted him and he exploded. She recognized the signs of addiction — all over again.[8]

.ࢽ   ࢽ   ࢽ

That individual men take pleasure in sexually stimulating pictures is disturbing, but even more disturbing is what those images teach men about sex, marriage, and women. The effects of the material are not limited to simple sexual arousal.

The first message of pornography is that sexual pleasure is the measure of the value of all activities and that women are mere objects of that gratification. Next, is that women *want* to be used this way. The "come hither" look of all the women in pornography displays that desire. But that desire, porn instructs, is often disguised, and the woman will resist the experience she actually desires.

It is here that one of the most common themes of pornography surfaces — *the rape myth* — the myth that women enjoy being forced (seduced, coerced, or even beaten) to engage in sex. This theme runs from the old B-grade movies where the hero takes hold of the resisting heroine, who until now has maintained her dislike for him, and kisses her. She pushes against him briefly but finally embraces him. In modern movie and TV fare, we have the likes of *9 1/2 Weeks* in which the man introduces a lonely, naive career woman to sado-masochism, bondage, and eventually rape — all of which she learns to thoroughly enjoy. All of this is mainstream filmmaking and is not even classed along with the pornography market. Graphic violence as a preliminary to graphic sex is the most common theme of the X-rated films and magazines.

Often it is argued that pornographic materials have little or no effect on behavior, but the multibillion-dollar-a-year advertising industry would be a sham if this were so. Advertising purposely attempts to link a product with happiness, fun, sex, or some other desirable end. The photographic images of people enjoying sex and/or sexual perversions affect people in a like manner.

In the first chapter, I showed that advertising was not an attempt to sell a *product* to *people* so much as it was the sale of *people* to a *producer.* In this light, pornography does not sell sex to people but people to Satan's skin trade. Satan's product, like that of Madame Babylon, is the bodies and souls of men. The enslavement of individual men does not satisfy him. He seeks to inundate the entire culture with false love and bring the entire culture into bondage.

Porno School

Imagine a young man who has grown up where the majority of his knowledge about sex comes from pornography or from the soft porn of most of today's mainstream movies.[9] This young man would believe that sex was only for pleasure — *his* own pleasure. In his mind there would be no connection between sex and marriage, commitment, love (even in the emotional sense), children, family, or anything outside his own enjoyment. In fact, pornography would teach him that there was not one whit of difference if he pleasured himself with someone of the same or opposite sex, an animal, or an inanimate object—so long as he enjoyed it.[10]

Sex education courses in public schools are of no use in offsetting this trend. After sex education, studies show, young people actually become *more tolerant* of deviant sex.[11]

Once again we must recall the intensity of the rape myth which is played like a one-note samba throughout pornography. How must that instill itself in his young mind? Add to that the usual modern preteen fare of "slasher" films where extreme and graphic violence is delivered to his ocular nerves immediately following the titillation of sexual suggestion.[12] Many young people are literally addicted to these films, which makes it possible for the societal pimps to sell the young audience to the skin trade using six or more badly produced sequels of the same horror. Is it any wonder the rape rate is unstoppable? As Franky Schaeffer once asked, "Do they still make millstones?"

But it is not just the vulnerable, unformed minds of the young that are seriously affected. Normal adult men are shown to have a lowered esteem of women after exposure to rape myth porn. Dr. Malamuth of UCLA, after exposing men to porn, asked them if they would rape a woman given that they would not be caught. Fifty-one percent of them answered, "Yes."[13]

Yet more startling are the studies that men are similarly affected by *nonviolent, consensual* pornographic material.[14]

Defenders of porn claim that the material actually has a *positive* effect. They point to Denmark and show that sex crimes were dramatically *reduced* after the legalization of pornography. What they do not reveal is that Denmark also decriminalized many sex crimes at the same time. Exposing one's self, fondling strangers, Peeping Tomism, certain kinds of sex with children, and many others were no longer illegal. The reduction of sex crimes dissolves into being a reduction of national conscience for the victims of these sex crimes.

Other lovers of porn claim that scientific research shows the *satiation* effect — the theory that pornography helps to release sexual tensions safely before they explode into some antisocial act. This is called the Catharsis Theory. The originator of the theory, Dr. Seymore Feshback, who originally proposed it in the fifties regarding television violence, has himself fully repudiated it after further study.[15]

The next surprise is that both men and women who are exposed to pornography showed a reduced sympathy for victims of rape. They were prone to view the rape victim as more responsible for her own plight. And this was a test involving nonviolent, consensual porn![16] Think of the effect on the justice system when these people serve on juries. While some porn addicts elect to become rapists, others dissolve their sympathy for rape victims with the corrosiveness of smut.

Men who use pornography regularly also see marriage as less valuable and less permanent.[17] Often, they demand that their wives perform the sexual gymnastics they see in the magazines and videos. In the early stages, while the addiction may be hidden from everyone including the wife, he will maneuver and cajole her into trying "something different." Later he may become more demanding, insisting that the sex acts of pornographic fantasy are normal and that "everybody does it this way." When wives refuse or fail to live up to the fantasy, the husbands will often turn to prostitutes.[18] Unbelievable pressure on marriages is generated this way. Many marriages are suspended in an awful stasis or are blown apart by the teachings of porn.

Women are trapped in the hideous cycle of alternately agreeing to watch and act out porn, then refusing—often to a fusillade of fists from an angry tantrum of their husbands. In other cases, men are ashamed of their degraded practices but find themselves woefully enslaved. These go to extraordinary lengths to hide their addiction. The dynamics of denial drive them deeper into depravity. Some men will seek to fulfill their frustrated fantasies with their children. The pandemic of sex crimes against children has closely followed the bounding advances in the acceptance of porn. As mentioned earlier, even soft porn magazines have used humor coupled with child pornography to teach the sexual use of children.[19]

The school of porn has taught misery and slavery.

Other Slaves

It would hardly be appropriate to leave the discussion of sexual slavery without mentioning the most visible and least recognized victims — the photographic subjects themselves. These pitiful remnants of humanity are often prostitutes and drug addicts who once willingly entered this sordid life. Now they are trapped.

Many times they are held by threat of beatings or at gunpoint. Even some of the "stars" of porn — those who appear to be basking in the fame and enjoying its riches — are shackled by fear of organized crime.[20] Organized crime often has "stables" of men, women, and children from which to draw their "stars."

Kidnapped or runaway children often end up as subjects for the burgeoning child porn trade. They spend years being passed around for photos, films, and prostitution. Sex becomes their entire world from childhood to adulthood.

But what is distressing is that the reason there are so many enslaved in *producing* pornography is that there are so many enslaved to *consuming* it.[21] All of this is based on a fantasy world. Helplessly, these victims stare down at the gaping, black pit of despairing death.

What We Have Seen

- Pornography is based on sexual fantasy.

- At first, porn was mostly written and increased with the advent of fast, cheap printing.

- Pornography was defended as love, beauty, nature, and art.

- The word *love* was expanded beyond emotion to encompass sex.

- Defenders of morality argued ineffectively because they, too, had accepted false premises.

- Even as pornography regulations grew, so did the apathy of law enforcement.

- As porn became associated with "art," it was viewed as a sophisticated form of expression.

- Many men were drawn into pornography through men's sophisticated magazines.

- Many men follow the pattern of addiction, escalation, desensitization, and acting out with pornography.

- Both men and women are negatively affected by pornographic exposure.

- These slaves of pornography often abuse their wives and children and destroy their marriages.

- Men, women, and children who are featured in pornography are virtual prisoners to the industry and are often kept by organized crime.

- The final frontier of pornography is the enslavement of children for sexual purposes.

What We Will See

The next track of the modern skin trade is prostitution. Prostitution is a twisted, debased form of marriage. It is brief, where marriage is lifelong; it is an exchange of money, where marriage is an exchange of vows of commitment; and it is sterile, where marriage is fruitful. The attraction of prostitution is the *illicitness* — the thrill of being out of bounds.

While harlotry has long been with civilized man, it has increased and abounded in new forms in the twentieth century. Where, in the past, prostitutes were more hidden, in this time they have become brazen — brazen to the point of starting "legitimate" organizations to promote their cause. The rationale for making prostitution acceptable to the public goes hand-in-hand with the sensual and naturalistic promotions of the skin trade.

6

FLESHPEDDLERS

The very word *prostitution* has a hiss of disdain. The dignity implied by the title, "the world's oldest profession," does not adhere to hooker, harlot, whore, or streetwalker. B-girl, hustler, and pickup all speak of the gutter, a tattered and frayed existence with a bold, glamorous facade. We see the street prostitute and we wince at the false flash and dash, the chintzy, glitzy, gaudy makeup and sequins.

Most of us think of things like this when we hear about prostitution. Yet the word *prostitute* really denotes using something good for corrupt or unworthy purposes. In this case, it is sex that is corrupted. This definition would have implications far beyond the streetwalker or high-priced call girl.[1] Nude or topless dancing, "modeling" for adult studios or pornography, dial-a-porn operators, and even a lot of advertising and mainstream movie-making are prostitution of God's gift of sex.

Mock Marriage

Prostitution is the epitome of Satan's ideal for marriage. It is brief, intense, self-gratifying, uncommitted, and anonymous. The very virtues that God intended for marriage have been ridiculed and parodied in prostitution. Where God called for a lifelong union, Satan has substituted quick sexual encounters. The unselfish giving called for in proper marriage is mocked by the single-minded drive for selfish pleasure. The demonic satire of the growing intimate knowledge of spouses is the anonymity of street sex.

In marriage, husband and wife establish a personal commitment between themselves and God. They exchange vows before members of the community. Faithfulness to those vows will ultimately benefit the whole community. In prostitution, all that is exchanged is money—in secret. The crass commercialism represents only an illicit transaction. Many who argue for legalization of prostitution will confidently assert that marriage is nothing more than a sex-for-support transaction. They will even say that it is a poor trade at that.[2] That anyone would even see a comparison between marriage and prostitution indicates how far the perverted satanic ideal has permeated the thoughts of Western man and may also indicate the state to which modern marriage has deteriorated.

God designed marriage to be fruitful in many ways—the most obvious being children and the corresponding responsibility for them. This responsibility is not found in the skin trade. The children who are not avoided or aborted by prostitutes are simply a tool to get government welfare money. There is certainly no responsibility — and probably no knowledge — on the part of the father.

Perennial Problems

There is certainly nothing new about prostitution. There have always been men and women willing to sell their heritage for a mess of pottage. But Western civilization was the first to actually try to curb the practice. It was viewed by Christians as a serious violation of God's order, and this concern was established in the minds of the general populace over many years.

Yet it was the rise of the naturalistic view of man that undercut the concern. Man, said the naturalists, was not just a bag of emotions but a bag of physical drives waiting to burst if not released. If one was hungry, it was argued, he ate; or thirsty, he drank. So, if he felt sexually stimulated, why not have sex? This idea gained sudden popularity with eager young men and humanist scientists. In a teaching similar to venting emotions, doctors and scientists posited that men *needed* sexual outlets. They pointed to nocturnal emissions as proof of this and said that if the men under pressure did not relieve themselves *immediately*, disaster would surely follow. These men, they insisted, must masturbate or find a prostitute (if they had no wife).

None of the naturalists bothered to explain why one could not simply leave the "release" to the nocturnal emissions. I suspect that the other methods were more to their liking.

This naturalistic approach to sex was used to excuse prostitution as a "necessary evil" for those unable to find a wife or those far from home when the pressure built up. No consideration was given to the proposal that the pressure was nothing more than simple lust. No one was encouraged to resist the urge to release the pressure. In fact, such resistance was presumed to be as dangerous as resisting to vent emotional pressure. With the rise of theories, like those of Margaret Mead, propounding that it was the restrictions of civilization that caused crime, this idea of danger in resisting release gained credibility.

Because of such thinking, sex soon became a natural right akin to other kinds of rights. If a wife did not have sex with her husband as often as (and later, in the particular *way*) he wanted, it was "perfectly understandable" that he might visit a prostitute or take on a mistress (a long-term prostitution arrangement, if there ever was one). This harked back to the pagan belief that it was natural for a young man to "sow his wild oats." It became a modern idiom that a man would take his son to a local prostitute for his initiation into the world of manhood (one wasn't a man until he had had sex). Sex was a *need* — a need on the order of food or water. But even then, every man seemed to want a virgin for his bride. Prostitutes and mistresses were still second-class women. A sordid double standard grew from the evil root of naturalistic sex. Since men's sex drive was more overt, naturalists seemed to think that sex was more natural for men than for women. It was almost as if the prostitute's real crime was *being unnatural.* In the nineteenth century, enforcement of prostitution laws was spotty and politically motivated. Rarely were the men implicated, unless it was to smudge the character of a political opponent. To read the reports, one would think that these women were having sex for money without the presence of men. It was all reminiscent of the woman brought to Jesus who had been caught in adultery, in the very act, *alone* (see John 8:1-11).

But even at the turn of the century, brash voices were being lifted for *female* sexual liberation. After all, if men were going to abandon their responsibilities in the sexual arena and wade in the hedonistic mire, women should be able to jump right in there and muck it up with them.

The most successful of these voices was Margaret Sanger, founder of Planned Parenthood. One of Sanger's chief goals, aside from eliminating "human weeds," was to free women from the "tyranny" of childbearing so they could be free to be the untrammeled sex objects of men like Havelock Ellis. This, she propounded, could be accomplished by unrestricted access to birth control and abortion.[3] The loss of the sanctity of love was beginning to chip away at the sanctity of life, but Sanger's siren call was still half a century from being answered.

Tolerance for Modern Slavery

Today, while most places retain their laws against prostitution, there is an underlying tolerance for it that allows the corruption to continue. The see-saw of public attention to the problem in local papers makes for "good" stories but little realistic action. Neighborhood groups scream loudly, but only that the scarlet women are marching the lanes of *their* area.

In one such furor over prostitution in Portland, Oregon, a neighborhood leader, who was leading the fight to stop the activity, was demanding that the police do something to get rid of the hookers. I commented to him that we needed to get rid of those, including the mayor, who wanted to legalize and zone prostitution. He replied, "I don't care, so long as the zone isn't in *my* neighborhood." This attitude is typical.

But in Europe things were different. In The Netherlands, prostitution is open and legal. Proponents crow that it has not created the predicted problems but rather benefits abound. Yet, like Denmark's brave claims about their hands-off policy on pornography, these "benefits" evaporate under scrutiny. Recent investigations have shown that many women who are prostitutes in The Netherlands were lured there from Asia, North and South America, and other parts of the world.

Once there and their money exhausted by the move, the jobs proved to be a sham, and they were forced into prostitution by those who had promised the employment. The skin trade flourishes there, and the same "solution" is regularly proposed for the U.S. Prostitute rights groups have sprung up to promote the decriminalization of the profession. One such organization, COYOTE (Call Off Your Old Tired Ethics)[4] epitomizes such efforts. Ex-hooker and organizer Margo St. James is a regular on the talk show circuit. Her cultivated appearance and disarming, flamboyant humor add appeal to the seemingly easy answer for a sexually hyperactive society.

The societal pimp tactic of using women like Margaret Sanger and Margaret Mead to promote sexual promiscuity among women (much to the delight of men) is mirrored in this fight to legalize prostitution. The National Organization for Women (NOW) promotes such legalization, though they use the argument that there is a difference between legalization and decriminalization and call for the latter. NOW has sold women into the slavery of careerism, selfism, promiscuity, abortion, lesbianism, and finally would have them selling themselves on the streets.

Adventures in the Skin Trade

Terri was an ancient nineteen. Her face was weathered by drugs taken too often, beatings taken too recently, years lived too fast, and cynicism grown too early. Her blonde hair was now straw-like and as lifeless as her eyes. She had been turning tricks since she was eleven years old.

At a glance, the pretty face that was hers was still visible — especially on the poorly lit Union Avenue with its backdrop of boarded, burnt-out buildings. She counted on her pretty face to sell her services. Most "johns" didn't look too closely anyway.

Bonnie and I walked up and introduced ourselves. "Here's a card with an emergency number — in case you want out of this. Take it. You never know when you'll need a 'back door.'"

Her eyes appeared to escape the drug stupor momentarily as she grabbed the business card for Friendship Unlimited, a prostitution alternative outreach. She knew *exactly* what I meant by a "back door."

A clot of cars approached and she craned her neck to see the drivers. Once again the drugged look covered her face like a pall. She was mesmerized by the traffic. Bonnie and I walked on praying for her. We would see her over the next few months on the street before she abruptly disappeared without a word.[5]

За   За   За

Many tentacles bind the prostitute — drugs, pimps, "the action," money, and "old friends." Of these, the strongest is "the action." Women may escape their pimp and old friends by moving; leave the drugs by entering the myriad public drug rehabilitation programs; the money needs will drop off significantly when drugs are eliminated. But "the action" is the intangible in their blood that makes the street — the trashy, ugly avenues — almost irresistibly beckon them to return. Despite the abusive pimps and "johns," the hurried, harried, round-the-clock hustle, the harassment of police and local residents, the miserable times in jail, the strung-out craving for drugs, and the frantic search for drug money which consumes most of their time, they still remember the street as "the good times."

The entry into prostitution is usually by choice — the lure of big money. These are runaways, throw-aways, and thrill seekers. Most often cited as the reason for children on the street is the incidence of sexual abuse in the home. Some quotes run as high as 95 percent. Recent Canadian studies question this, showing only one-sixth motivated by sexual abuse (the most common runaways' reasons being continuous family fighting and alcoholic fathers).[6]

But still, most entered the trade *voluntarily* for the fast, easy cash.[7] For most, this is the bait. The switch comes when they are emaciated, diseased addicts selling their wasted wares for a pittance to feed their habits. The excitement, the fun, the thrill of the illicit all combine to mesmerize them while the bonds are strapped on. Drugs dull the pain of abusive "johns" and pimps. Their eye is fixed on the fantasy of future wealth, fame, ease, and power. Even as they slide down the slope to inhumanity, they still believe — the fantasy reigns.

How Much Is That Child
in the Window?

You walk the cobblestone streets of old Amsterdam past the ancient shops that once held watch repair shops, dressmakers, and tinkers. Large plate glass windows before the display racks have now replaced the leaded diamond panes of earlier times.

You look at the display in the centuries-old, gray stone shop. Inside, on a divan that has seen better times, are seated several women. Behind are a few more — smoking cigarettes and casually looking out at you with hooded eyes. All are in various states of undress, wearing bits and pieces of lingerie.

These are this shop's wares.

With a start, you realize that some of these "women" are mere children — kids who should be passing notes in sophomore algebra class. You remember that the age of consent here is sixteen. Whether these girls are sixteen or not, they are certain to have identity papers showing they are.

"They are selling their children," you think in utter dismay. *"At least our age of consent is higher in the U.S."*

&a.   &a.   &a.

A twenty-two-year-old Patterson, New Jersey woman has been charged with getting girls as young as ten hooked on the drug crack and then forcing them to become prostitutes for the drugs.

The woman was held on charges that she got as many as eight girls addicted to the powerful cocaine derivative. She then sent them out as prostitutes nearly every day in a poor, drug-ridden area of town.

Mayor Frank Graves of Patterson said, "America has hit the bottom of the barrel."[8]

‰   ‰   ‰

Portland, Oregon, once touted as the Most Livable City in the U.S., is also known nationally as "Boys Town" because of the availability of very young male prostitutes for rent or sale.

‰   ‰   ‰

"Grasshopper," as he is known for the frenetic pace he keeps in his day job hawking restaurant coupon books, beckons to the driver with a lewd gesture.

A Cabbagetown son with the mannerly "yessirs" inbred by the Georgia state prison system, Grasshopper approaches the car. The driver senses something *right* about him and stops for conversation.

After a few minutes of negotiation, Grasshopper jumps in the car.

For sex. For money.[9]

‰   ‰   ‰

One of the indisputable facts of sexual slavery is that people, particularly men, quickly tire of the same old thing and begin seeking more exotic forms for their gratification. Man's natural attraction for young women of childbearing age is one of the things that is distorted when a man blindly stumbles down the path of deviancy. He begins to desire younger and younger women for his sexual pleasure. For a time, he may be satisfied with women who deliberately dress as girls in their early teens or who naturally look juvenile. There is a premium on such prostitutes; they command higher prices. But the degenerating "customer" soon knows — to his sexual dissatisfaction — that it is a ruse.

He feels that he needs actual young girls for his pleasures. The market is only too happy to comply — for a price. But even this soon wears thin as the young girls provided are as experienced and casual about the whole thing as the older pro on the street, and his desire finally focuses on his *real* target — innocence. Like the temptation to soil the smooth whiteness of a new snowfall, now his drive — as is Satan's — is the destruction of innocence, which is the precursor of all virtue.

What We Have Seen

- Prostitution is the use of anything for corrupt or unworthy purposes.

- Sexual prostitution is the selling of one's self for the sexual gratification of another.

- Street prostitution and call-girl prostitution are mockeries of God's design in marriage.

- Where marriage is until death, prostitution is for the moment.

- Where marriage implies intimate knowledge, prostitution thrives on anonymity.

- Where marriage is an exchange of profound vows, prostitution is an exchange of cash.

- Where marriage demands commitment, prostitution is implacable.

- Where marriage intends fruitfulness, prostitution exults in barrenness.

- Powerful male sex drives virtually insure the existence of prostitution.

- Naturalism (with its man-as-bag doctrine) justified the need for the male release of sexual energies.

- The influence of the noble savage myth encouraged sex as a natural act of natural man.

- Margaret Mead and other scientists "proved" that societies with liberated sex practices were healthier than societies which were "repressed" by codes of morality, for example, Christianity. This was the sociological mirroring of the Freudian psychology and naturalistic physiology.

- As a result, prostitution became a tolerated "necessary evil" which was often used by society to release sexual energies and "make a man" of pubescent males.

- While prostitution was accepted as a necessary evil, the women themselves were viewed as necessarily evil and treated as second-class people.

- While prostitution legalization proponents crow about freedom, most prostitutes are enslaved to numerous things — not the least of which are the abusive men who "own" them.

- Women in prostitution generally start willingly for the fast cash but are soon trapped. Drug and alcohol addiction plays a major part in their enslavement, though it is often "the action" that keeps them blinded to their slavery and coming back for more.

- Prostitutes who stay in the business usually wind up dying young through the agency of drugs, many beatings, and just plain wearing out.

- As prostitution increases and becomes more common, the "customers" begin to demand better (i.e., younger) prostitutes.

- This demand increases the price for sex with minors and leads to an ever increasing pressure to lower age of consent laws. It also creates a market for even parents to sell their own children.

What We Will See

Before looking at the overall sexual revolution of the twentieth century, the next chapter will look at what was once considered an aberration (even by sexual libertines) but has become a key player — the homosexual movement.

The development of acceptability for this perversion, like pornography, ran concurrently with the rest of the revolution, but there are significant differences that deserve separate treatment.

When emotions became accepted as reliable guiding forces, it almost precluded acceptance of eccentric behavior among artists who, after all, were more *sensi-*

tive than the rest of us. Creative people, it was believed, were *always* in touch with their feelings, and thus, their peculiarities were not only forgivable but expected. Effeminacy became one of the popular affectations of the "creative."

Thus homosexuality began to attain acceptability through the arts. Later it joined the rest of the revolution — even to becoming militant.

7

SODOM REVISITED

It was about 1 A.M. Bonnie and I strolled together up the darkened avenue in southwest Portland. The light from the doorway of the homosexual "bath house" flung itself across our path as the door swung open. We slowed our pace, wondering what was in store for us in this sordid district.

A middle-aged man boldly stepped out, a young man of about fourteen years in tow. The tall, well-dressed man was brought up short by our presence and averted his eyes from Bonnie's steady look. His hand still holding the arm of the boy, he began to distractedly edge toward the silver Mercedes parked curbside directly before the door of the business.

The boy's look as he was led into the passenger seat was half pleading and half the fearful look of the hunted. Darkness enveloped the two as the "bath house" door eased closed. The older man quickly took his place in the leather seat behind the wheel, fired up the engine, and pulled away.

It was over in less than ten seconds. The haunted boy was gone.[1]

     ta.   ta.   ta.

"We shall sodomize your sons. . . . " (Michael Swift, a homosexual activist)[2]

     ta.   ta.   ta.

How blessed and favored you are that God has made you Gay! He has given you an honor that far exceeds that of childbearing. He has exalted you above the angels by giving you a place in heaven that is the highest among men. He has given you a heavenly song that only you can sing. (*An open letter to a gay Christian*, Father Thomas, Everett, Washington)[3]

     ta.   ta.   ta.

In the Christian West, homosexuality was always considered sin. Even with the advent of romanticism, homosexuals gained no ground because what they did was widely excluded from the term *love*. Homosexuals[4] carefully hid their activities from others for the rightful fear of legal and ecclesiastical sanction. Claims of a constant 10 percent of humanity being homosexual to the contrary, homosexuality was extremely rare. The lack of communications and a network made large numbers impossible. Such sexual activity would of necessity have limited itself primarily to the wealthy and powerful who would be able to mask their participation.

Without access to the deceptive version of love, the homosexuals were seen as merely perverted. The church offered the hope of salvation through repentance. A prime example was Augustine, who had engaged in every kind of perverseness before his conversion and had gone on to become one of the pillars of the early church. But the church also regarded continuing homosexuality as dangerous to all of society. It correctly observed that acceptance of homosexuality was not only a sign of moral decay but also of imminent judgment from God. (This view was later vindicated by the researches of the historian, Toynbee.) Greece and Rome were displayed as models of this pattern.

But the influence of romanticism, which exalted feeling over reason, also distorted the vocation of the artist. Instead of being seen as a person of discipline, artists suddenly were visualized as creatures of whim with an indefinable income of "talent" that accounted for their work. The growth of the concept of artist as captured by emotions lent itself to excusing peculiarities—and even outright sin—as "artistic temperament" ("Well, my dear, don't you know—he's an *artist!*"). In the past it was believed that real individuality expressed itself, not in affectations, but in the judicious application of abilities and talents. Soon it was fashionable for an artist to strive outside his art for distinctives to express "individuality." Affectations of behavior, dress, or appearance were regarded as *prima facie* evidence of artistic talent. For them, allowances were made.

And as artists strove for more high profile affectations, effeminacy and homosexuality grew in the artistic community.

The Naturalist and the Unnatural

When naturalistic science fully blossomed, the scientists found a great difficulty with the homosexual. Though a strong sex drive was instantly recognized as natural (and thus, good), the practices of the homosexual were distinctly unnatural. They were in a quandary as to whether to try to cure the sodomite or to embrace him — in the nonphysical sense, of course. Mostly, they came to a tacit agreement to theorize about him and otherwise leave him alone. Freud rescued the beleaguered scientists. He did this by positing that homosexuality was merely a healthy sex drive distorted by childhood trauma and a moralistic unconscious.

Again, it was morality itself that was to blame. Homosexuality, while viewed as a distortion of nature, was freed from the harsh moral judgment of being called sin. Few looked beyond the surface of the vile practice to imagine where these men were getting their supply of sex partners. Naturalistic psychiatrists treated homosexuality in a vacuum without regard to the young men who were being lured or forced into the practice. They were so intent on the personal childhood traumas of the homosexual that they entirely overlooked the shattered childhoods of the homosexual's victims.

In most cases, homosexuality was regarded as harmless because knowledge of the nature of homosexual practices was studiously avoided. Most people thought a *pansy* was just a man who acted feminine and who perhaps kissed other feminine men. Anal sex and other perversities were quite beyond the ken of the average person. Failure to acknowledge the unclean and abominable practice — and then to condemn it — only served to encourage its growth.

The Pleasure Principle

"I am seriously distressed," Jade McCall, homosexual writer, penned about the sodomite community's response to the AIDS epidemic, "by the increasing number of gay persons, leaders and publications which seem horrified when recalling the sexual explorations of the 1970s. . . .

"I don't regret the sex I enjoyed in the '70s and early '80s. I eagerly experienced the opportunities offered by the sexual revolution, emerging gay rights and related choices. . . .

"It was great! I believe that all sex is great — intimate or anonymous, romantic or furtive, playful or deviant. I loved it all and I did it all as often as I could, especially the adventurous, playful, and deviant. . . .

"Romance, monogamy and cerebral relationships are different from promiscuity and sexual exploration. But they are not better nor more moral. 'Unhealthy and dangerous' are not the same as 'evil and wrong.'"[5]

ᘈ   ᘈ   ᘈ

Jade's view did not develop in a vacuum. The primary principle in these statements is that all that Jade and others like him did during those years of total abandon to sexual exploration is justified by the fact that it was pleasurable. If it feels good, do it! If it felt good, it was right. No matter that many of the *gay* brothers and sisters so publicly mourned with quilts and ACT/UP[6] demonstrations are dead as a result of that attitude.

This is the point where the growth in homosexuality joins the decline of the sexual liberation movement. The pleasure principle had been gaining ground for about a century but was mostly unacceptable to the public until the post-war years, especially in America. The rigors of war over, the boys from overseas just wanted to get back home and relax a bit. But the bit turned into something more long term when the goal became *a pleasant life.* And a pleasant life came to be epitomized in the quiet materialism of the fifties.

The growing children of the fifties were steeped in this passive corrosive. In the sixties, these young rebelled against the apathy and indifference of their parents. Yet, sacrifice and selflessness was not the long suit of these trained hedonists, and they soon found their own pleasant life — living off others, taking drugs, and having sex, sex, sex. Where their parents were content with a good income for minimal work, three martinis, and one spouse (and the occasional affair), these young had defined pleasure on their own terms. And who was to say they were wrong? Outside of "This is the way we've *always* done it," and "Well, it just ain't right," the parents didn't have any real moral ground to stand on. Besides, these little geniuses had been told from kindergarten that they were "the smartest generation ever on earth," and their college professors, at parents' expense, instructed them how to debate their parents' drudgery of morals into the dust.

Dad had bought *Playboy* since it first hit the newsstands, but that was a secret obsession (Mom knew, but she pretended not to). Son had surreptitiously checked out the centerfolds, but now called his father a hypocrite and headed for the nearest love-in.

The hippie movement capitalized on *love*. Love was what the world needs now — love was all you needed — *everything* was love!

Alongside the love buttons appeared fluorescent tabs saying "Gay is good" and "God is gay." Most people simply assumed the old meaning of *gay* as happy, but it wasn't long before talk of *gay* love was injected into the love-charged atmosphere. The wild abandon and the drug-induced fervor of the sexual orgies of the time lent themselves to shameless experimentation. Under the careless guidance of gurus like Janis Joplin singing, "You know you got it — if it makes you feel good," morals fell like ninepins.

New beings called *bisexuals* came into existence. Even the heterosexuals wore their *de rigueur* tolerance like a badge. "I don't care if people are homosexual so long as they don't mess with me," they chanted, not thinking of the young victims of homosexual recruitment. No one could think of a valid reason for denying them their pleasure — except a few religious fanatics

122 ROMANCED TO DEATH

who kept warning that the sodomites would next want
to teach their practices in the public schools. But no
one listened to nuts like that. Besides they were doing
so well at being *tolerant* — it was the *loving* thing to
do, after all. All moral energy dissipated in the face of
love defined as pleasure. The homosexuals had found
the perfect moral solvent — love.

Pretty Political in Pink

The first order of business is *desensitization* of the
American public concerning gays and gay rights. To
desensitize the public is to help it view homosexuality with indifference instead of with keen emotion.
Ideally, we would have straights register differences
in sexual preference in the way they register different tastes for ice cream: she likes strawberry and I
like vanilla; he follows baseball and I follow foot-
ball. No big deal.

At least in the beginning, we are seeking public desensitization *and nothing more.* . . . You can forget
about trying to persuade the masses that homosexuality is a *good* thing. But if only you can get them
to think it is just *another* thing, with a shrug of their
shoulders, then your battle for legal and social rights
is virtually won. (Emphasis in original)[7]

The first goal was *tolerance*, but tolerance would
not be enough. It must move from there to acceptance,
to affirmation, to applause. In fact, the article from
which the above quote is taken, in their own words,

"sketched out . . . a blueprint for transforming the social values of straight America." The steps fit very well over the blueprint for seduction discussed in the first two chapters of this book. But these skills were learned and honed in the early years when homosexuals marched side-by-side with leftist political groups.

Having found a home in the sexually liberated hippie movement, the transition into politics was simple. At first, in the sixties, they banded together with the antiwar groups, the free speech groups, and civil rights groups in the political mayhem of the time.

Enviously, they watched others having their demands met. It was not long before they realized that they, too, could have a political agenda. At first, it was rather modest—just let us alone to live in peace. But seeing the blacks and women attaining *minority* status and special rights, the homosexual leaders focused on this new goal. It would have been hard to mobilize the homosexual community but for the police departments in some large cities which still regularly raided known homosexual hangouts.

On one fateful raid, an illegal alien homosexual died from a fall off a fire escape. Anger rumbled through the homosexual ranks of New York City, and when police raided the Stonewall Bar in late June of 1969, the homosexual patrons erupted into two days of violence and street tension.[8]

This incident galvanized many homosexual activists. Their political experiences with the other protest groups were brought to bear as they began demanding

that police leave them alone. Powerfully placed homosexuals and other liberals lobbied heavily in city halls
and state legislatures for the repeal—or at least ignoring—of sodomy laws.

The first major break came when, in 1973, the
American Psychiatric Association (APA) *voted* homosexuality out of the list of psychiatric disorders. From
thence, the only psychiatric disorder related to homosexuality was *egodystonic homosexuality* in which
someone had mental difficulties stemming from his in-
ability to accept his own homosexuality. The only
problem, the psychiatrists said, was not being able to
overcome repugnance and guilt for your own acts. But
the APA outdid itself in 1986 by voting that even this
self-loathing was no longer a problem, thus abandon-
ing the homosexuals to permanent misery.[9]

Of course, it would be hard to convince the average person to accept homosexuals if their disgusting
sexual practices were spotlighted. So, in a handbook
on marketing the homosexual community to the public,
the author said plainly, "Instead, the imagery of sex
should be downplayed, and gay rights should be reduced to an abstract social question as much as possible. First let the camel get his nose inside the tent—
and only later his unsightly derriere."[10]

The "Unsightly Derriere"

"Healthy Sex" the pamphlet trumpeted. Upon opening
the brochure, the bold headlines stood out: "F——ing,

S— —ing, Kissing." Under each was an extremely colloquial description of how to safely engage in each sexual act. The drawings were of distinctly effeminate men (or odd couples) "with" each other. Smaller headlines described dildoes (artificial or mechanical penises), water sports (urinating on one another), rimming (oral/anal contact), and fisting (inserting fists and arms into rectums).

These pamphlets were widely distributed to the public and public schools and were produced by a tax-exempt, tax-supported AIDS project.[11]

        ᵃ   ᵃ   ᵃ

The pedophile organization, National Man/Boy Love Association (NAMBLA), which promotes the elimination of all age-of-consent laws for sex, marches yearly in the New York City Gay and Lesbian Pride parade.

New York's Mayor Koch never failed to join the parade.

        ᵃ   ᵃ   ᵃ

SAN DIEGO, Calif. (AP) — A judge awarded custody of a 16-year-old boy to his late father's homosexual lover yesterday, saying the youth would have the "stable and wholesome environment" his fundamentalist Christian mother could not provide. . . . Under the ruling, Brian will continue to live in Palm Springs with Craig Corbett, who sought custody after Brian's father, Frank, died of an AIDS-related illness in June.[12]

೩.   ೩.   ೩.

OAKLAND, Calif. (AP)—Two men who posed as husband and wife while adopting a 14-month-old boy were charged with the infant's murder after they admitted beating him, police said Tuesday.

The unemployed men had been caring for the baby since April and apparently were cleared by a private adoption agency after required background checks, authorities said.

Police Sgt. Jerry Harris said, however, that neighbors had warned the agency it was giving the baby to two men.[13]

೩.   ೩.   ೩.

BOSTON, Mass. (UP)—The Boston Police Department, responding to criticism from a gay rights group, said Friday that it would recruit homosexual and lesbian candidates before the next police entrance exams.[14]

೩.   ೩.   ೩.

PORTLAND, Ore.—Gay rights demonstrators marched outside Portland Foursquare Church Sunday—then interrupted the service inside—in protest of the passage last week of Measure 8.

The measure repealed Governor Neil Goldschmidt's order that banned discrimination on the basis of sexual orientation. Opponents of the measure noted Foursquare leaders actively encouraged their congregations to vote in favor of the measure.[15]

✺   ✺   ✺

The alliance of leftist political groups with the homosexual groups continues. Equating homosexuality with race and calling for civil rights for homosexuals is the most common ploy. This connection is clearly demonstrated by the popular leftist chant against conservatives, "Racist, sexist, anti-gay, / Born-again bigots, go away!"

But more quietly, homosexuals are gaining subtle ground in government administrative regulations and resolutions which later advance to ordinances and state laws.

Nondiscrimination laws in cities and counties have been foisted on cowed politicians. The state of Oregon legislature passed a bill making it a felony to harass a homosexual.[16] San Francisco's Board of Supervisors unanimously adopted an ordinance legally recognizing "domestic partnerships" of either sex for the purposes of insurance, ownership, and other rights accorded to married couples.[17] West Hollywood, a new city created by a vote of the largely homosexual population, elected a lesbian mayor and an almost entirely homosexual city council. This council passed a law which eliminated Christmas vacation for employees in order to do away with holidays with Christian religious overtones.[18]

But the greatest help in the campaign for special status (besides the ACLU) is the crisis caused by the appearance of AIDS. This gave the homosexual more opportunity for exposure as a victim than anything heretofore. While screaming that AIDS was "not a homosexual disease," they used the epidemic to garner special rights and treatment at taxpayers' expense. People who called diseased homosexuals to account for their sins were played in the media as unfeeling bigots who picked on "handicapped" people.[19] The victim strategy has been enormously enhanced by *using* the AIDS crisis to their own advantage. So effective has the homosexual rights' campaign been while joined to the disease, that AIDS has been said to be the only disease with civil rights.

For all of the tears shed over the dying AIDS "victims," action by the homosexual community to close "bath houses" or cease public sexual stimulation through homosexual erotica in the form of printed "phone sex" ads has been curiously lacking.

Homosexual Sales Pitch

"Talk about gays and gayness. . . . The principle behind this advice is simple: almost any behavior begins to look normal if you are exposed to enough of it. . . . People featured in the public campaign should be upright, appealing and admirable by straight standards. . . . Our campaign should not demand direct support for homo*sexual* practices, but should instead take *anti-discrimination* as its theme. . . . the campaign should paint gays as *superior* pillars of society. Yes, yes, we know — this trick is so old it creaks. . . . At a later stage of the media campaign for gay rights it will be time to get tough with remaining opponents. To be blunt, they must be vilified. . . . These images might include . . . bigoted southern ministers drooling with hysterical hatred." ("The Overhauling of Straight America")[20]

    ха.   ха.   ха.

"We shall sodomize your sons. . . . If you dare cry faggot, fairy or queer, at us, we will stab you in your cowardly hearts and defile your dead, puny bodies. . . . The family unit will be abolished. . . . All churches who condemn us will be closed. . . . Those who oppose us will be exiled. . . . We shall rewrite history. . . . We are the natural aristocrats. . . . Any man contaminated by heterosexual lust will be automatically barred from a position of influence. . . . We too are capable of firing guns and manning the barricades of the ultimate revolution. Tremble, hetero swine, when we appear before you without our masks." (Michael Swift, homosexual activist)[21]

    ха.   ха.   ха.

Perhaps more deliberately than any other group in the sexual revolution, the homosexual groups have a fixed agenda and a solid plan. Earlier in the chapter, and above, I quoted from "The Overhauling of Straight America," a detailed map of the homosexuals' route to respectability — and eventually to exalted status in Western culture.

Like the seductions described in chapters 1 and 2, this plan depends first on getting attention, though not in a lustful way, and drawing in the customer with a false or fantasy image of what is being presented. In other words, the classic bait-and-switch — capture the attention of the public with the civil rights' plight of a group of normal-looking people who were allegedly born homosexual. When the package is bought, it contains bizarre-looking people who engage in disgusting and unsanitary acts for sexual thrills and whose only means of growth is recruitment of the young.

As you read the following portion, keep in mind that this is the outline for a massive *sales* campaign — a sales campaign that is selling Western civilization further into the skin trade.

Tip number one from this outline is: "Talk about gays and gayness as loudly and often as possible." This, for the purposes of this book, could be likened to *the look* or getting the attention. Under this section, the authors explain what we all have heard in verse.

> Vice is a creature of such frightful mien
> As to be hated, needs but to be seen.
> Yet seen too oft, familiar with her face
> We first endure, then pity, then embrace.[22]

The authors of the blueprint for homosexual rights immediately point out that "the imagery of sex should be downplayed and gay rights should be reduced to an abstract social question."

Hollywood exposure is considered most desirable, even though the vehicle of exposure is sometimes comedy. All the *talk*, they say, should desensitize the public. Here again the original meaning for amusement (mentioned in chapter 3) comes into play since most television is specifically designed to entertain without engaging the mind.

Second on the agenda, "Overhauling" recommends: •
"Portray gays as victims, not aggressive challengers." This is the bait of the bait-and-switch sale, or the fantasy part of seduction. Here the writers advise deceit by not showing homosexuals as "a strong and prideful tribe." They continue, "We must forgo the temptation to strut our 'gay pride' publicly when it conflicts with the Gay Victim image." They warn that the National Man/Boy Love Association be moved to the background "while sympathetic figures of nice young people, old people, and attractive women would be featured."

As part of the "victim" package, they say, "The mainstream should be told that gays are *victims of fate,* in the sense that most never had a choice to accept or reject sexual preference." The homosexual-by-birth lie is encouraged and carefully perpetrated with the implication that "These folks are victims of a fate that could have happened to me."

To round it out, the authors suggest that homosexuals be portrayed as "*victims of society.*" Part of this included recent releases by the obviously biased National Gay and Lesbian Task Force — but accepted as virtually scientific by the media — showed "alarming increases" in "violence against gays." Since this "task force" has not been studying the issue long enough to make a comparison, the "study" has little real credibility but enormous media marketability. Included in the term *violence* were such things as name-calling — of the

7,248 incidents, almost 5,000 were verbal. Out of the seventy murders of homosexuals, twenty-two were classified as "anti-gay."[23] What is never shown is that many homosexual deaths are self-inflicted by their growing participation in sadomasochistic activities.

In the bait-and-switch business, the next move is to get the target emotionally linked to the product and psychologically linked to the purchase. In very real terms, the customer comes to the store mentally prepared to buy and with a precarious happiness balanced on his ability to walk away having discharged his "need." Similarly, the victim strategy emotionally connects the "unfortunate" homosexual to his heterosexual counterpart by presenting *gay rights* as a compelling need. The next step is to show the heterosexual how he can help meet this "need."

"Overhauling's" authors suggest: "Give protectors a just cause." This is to help heterosexuals overcome their last hesitation and commit themselves to *some kind* of action. It need not be overt, but it will give them a stake in the outcome. It is common knowledge that when someone has committed time or money to something that the links become nearly unbreakable.

The "just cause," say the authors, is civil rights. "Our campaign," they say, "should not demand direct support for homo*sexual* practices. . . . The right of free speech, freedom of beliefs, freedom of association, due process and equal protection of laws—these should be the concerns. . . . It is especially important for the gay movement to hitch its cause to accepted standards of law and justice . . . " (emphasis in the original).

Americans, steeped in the rightness of *rights* will be willing to be protective toward homosexual *victims* — and without realizing it, will be protecting a foothold of perversity in their own society.

Much like the seductress in Proverbs 7 and her glowing descriptions of her boudoir and the pleasures within, much like the adman's pitch of the good or pleasure of owning his advertised product, the homosexual pitchmen in "Overhauling" flatly state: "Make gays look good."

Again, still masking the true nature of homosexuality, they recommend displaying various famous men and women whom they allege to have been homosexual. They do not suggest offering *proof* of these assertions, since it would probably interfere with the simplicity of the lie — and might even cause someone to *think*. They say, "In no time, a skillful and clever media campaign could have the gay community looking like the veritable fairy godmother to Western civilization."

In fact, in the Michael Swift diatribe quoted at the heading of this segment, the claim is made, "We will demonstrate that homosexuality and intelligence are inexorably linked, and that homosexuality is a requirement for true nobility, true beauty in man."

But when someone is demonstrating the beauty of seduction, it is also helpful to contrast it with the ugliness — or at least drabness — of the alternative. In sales it helps to point out the drudgery—and even unfairness—of life without the product. It is in this spirit that "Overhauling's" writers advise next: "Make victimizers look bad."

They explain, "The public should be shown images of ranting homophobes whose secondary traits and beliefs disgust middle America. These images might include . . . the Ku Klux Klan."

Another method of neutralizing homosexual opposition is the development of a new psychological disease of *homophobia*. Once this becomes accepted by the American Psychiatric Association as a *psychological disorder* it may even be possible to imprison antigays in psychiatric hospitals out of "compassion." Sounds like re-education—Gulag-style.

What You See Is What You Get

Little Billy, like thousands of other school-aged, latchkey children, let himself in the house and flicked on the TV as he went to drop off his books in his Star Wars decor bedroom. On the trip back, he dumped out a bowl-full of nacho chips, grabbed an apple, and headed back to the living room where the old Zenith was just ending its typical warm-up horizontal roll.

The music and color caught his attention and signaled the beginning of his favorite show—the CBS "Schoolbreak Special." This one was entitled, "What if

I'm Gay?" Billy wrinkled his eleven-year-old brow, not knowing what to make of the title. As the show progressed, the title became abundantly clear. And even though alone, Billy blushed and squirmed when the realization dawned; it gave him a funny feeling all over. He was even more uncomfortable as he recalled disconcerting feelings he'd had when changing into his swimsuit last summer at the public pool. But just as he was about to shut the TV off for embarrassment, the school counselor on the show spoke to young Todd, the macho soccer team captain, who was upset about his sexual feelings for other boys. The counselor was reassuringly saying, "Todd, if you are homosexual, it doesn't mean your life is over, or you're condemned to some bleak, perverted existence. All it means is that you're going to be living a different lifestyle. And there's no reason it can't be very dignified and fulfilling. You can fall in love and you can be as happy as you want to be."

Billy relaxed a little.[24]

δ&   δ&   δ&

According to two homosexual authors, 73 percent of homosexuals have had sex with boys sixteen to nineteen *and younger*.[25]

δ&   δ&   δ&

In Marlin, Texas, police recently discovered that Jimmy Etheridge may have molested as many as 54 young, poor minority boys. Most of the children found in a list of the names and addresses in a computer kept by Etheridge, along with details about sexual relations he had with them, were hispanic or black between thirteen and sixteen years old at the time of contact with him.[26]

&   &   &

In New York, homosexuals support sex between teachers and students "as long as it occurs outside the classroom."[27]

&   &   &

The "closet activities" of Ted Washburn, one of the most experienced teachers at the Buckingham, Browne, and Nichols private school in Boston, were recently brought to light. Washburn sexually abused two boys. Both were students at the school. A third student was unsuccessfully propositioned by him.

Washburn brought the children unescorted, with parents' permission, to his family's summer home in Squam Lake in New Hampshire, where he made *Playboy* and *Penthouse* available to them. Washburn also encouraged some boys to visit his own home, where he also made *Playboy* and *Penthouse* available.[28]

&   &   &

"We shall sodomize your sons." (Michael Swift)

&   &   &

If sex is for pleasure, why any restrictions? This is the ultimate question of the pervert. And, given the presumption, the conclusion would be correct.

Homosexuals often complain about discrimination on the basis of "who we love" meaning "who we have sex with." This is an ultimate distortion of love as it is Biblically defined — and even a distortion of the romantic literature version. None of the vile practices of homosexuals were the province of love in either venue. Homosexuals have only one way to "reproduce," and it is not through "love" but by exploitation of the young. A thorough reading of the article by Michael Swift (reprinted in entirety in the endnotes of chapter 1) can convince anyone of this intention. The homosexual community support of National Man/Boy Love Association is another indicator. One homosexual activist says, "If it were not for our society's almost psychotic fear of sex, no one would get upset about a *consensual* sexual relationship between an adult and someone who is 'under age.'" This writer goes on to say:

> It is important that the gay community not abandon the most unpopular and socially despised segment of our community — i.e., man-boy lovers. . . . Sex is a pleasurable activity and it is hard to see what harm is done to the child if the child has slept with an adult of his or her own free will.[29]

As mentioned earlier, sex education courses serve to increase *tolerance and acceptance* of deviant sexual practices. Add to that the new AIDS and sex education curriculum which, by necessity, will have to teach homosexual relations. What a coup for the sodomites! This way they not only recruit young boys for their seduction, but they capture a whole generation in sympathy for their perversion. If the next several groups of children through grade school are thus brainwashed, in twenty years the nation will be a plum for all perverts.

Already, pedophile groups are releasing "scientific" studies showing that children are better adjusted when they have sex with adults. Other tests are alleged to show that the body cavities of four-year-old children are suitable for intercourse. The Rene Guyon Society, a pedophile group based in California, lobbies with these "studies" and the motto, "Sex before eight or it's too late." In one of their magazines they reported, "The (anal) cavity is large enough at age 4 for both girls and boys to painlessly hold an adult penis — an act they constantly desire from the adult males they love."[30] Their British equivalent, The Pedophilic Information Exchange, suggests four as the age of consent.[31] If childhood can be destroyed and they can come to believe that life itself consists of sex, the barbarians from within will have won.

What We Have Seen

- Homosexuality was considered a perversion. It was not included under even the distorted definition of *love*.

- The romantic era produced a belief that artists were naturally peculiar. One of these peculiarities was effeminism and homosexuality.

- Under this belief, homosexuality was justified or at least tolerated.

- Naturalistic psychiatry viewed homosexuality as a normal sex drive perverted by a moralistic subconscious. Homosexuality was regarded as a mostly harmless psychological disorder.

• When the 1960s came, many homosexuals used the "free sex" movement and the popularity of "love" to begin revealing themselves.

• Homosexuals learned political tactics while helping the anti-war, free speech, and women's rights' groups.

• Their consolidated learning has given them a plan for seducing Western civilization that is a textbook seduction technique from Proverbs 7 as well as being a classic bait-and-switch sales technique.

• In the modern confusion over love being emotion *and* sex, this sales job has been highly successful among legislators and influential people.

• The goals of the homosexual movement are absolute control of the culture and the government.

• The final, and most important step, is to gain control of the minds of today's grade-schoolers through sex education and AIDS education.

What We Will See

The next chapter looks at the overall effects of the sexualization and seduction of modern Western society. American culture is so sexualized that it is literally led "as an ox" from one perversion to the next.

Movie-makers claim that what shocks theatergoers today will be acceptable on television in about five years, clearly indicating the decline. Sex revolutionaries, however, claim that these are signs of a growing, healthy culture.

The pulse of our "growing, healthy culture" is moribund, adrift in a scummy, backwater eddy where life is ultimately measured by only one thing—sex.

8

THE MODERN MIRE: BEING LED AS AN OX

In the late afternoon, she went back to the hotel and went to bed. "I only had 40p [pence] left and I didn't know anybody." The very next morning she found out what London meant to a thirteen-year-old on the run. "The hotel man came in my room at eight o'clock. He didn't even knock, he just used his passkey. He said I owed over fifteen pounds. I said, 'My God, I only have 40p left.' I was so stupid, I thought I had to tell him — I thought it would be dishonest not to. I said, could I work it off? I asked him whether I could clean rooms in his hotel till I found a job. He said," she laughed bitterly, "you know what the b — —-d said? He said, 'I'm not allowed by law to employ you — you are underage.' Of course, he could see I was. I looked a kid — my God, did I just. Anyway, he said I shouldn't be silly, that it was easy to make money. This was *London,* man, he said, and I wasn't a bad looker. He reckoned I ought to be able to make a hundred pounds a day without trying. Yes, I knew what he meant. My mum had told me often enough I'd end up a whore."[1]

      ❧   ❧   ❧

I saw the faces of those children. I sat for hours and watched those children.

I will never get away from that as long as I shall live. In my film series *Turn Your Heart Toward Home* I made reference to one particular film of a little boy who had been abducted by a molester. And the molester took his picture and then these pictures were confiscated when they caught him.

This little boy was nine years of age. He had blonde hair — kind of a cute little haircut. In the first picture he was alive and hc was clothed — and for some reason, he was smiling.

And in the second picture — I will never forget — he was nude and dead . . . and had a butcher knife in his chest.[2]

      ❧   ❧   ❧

We are jaded. If we had heard these stories twenty years ago we would have vomited. We also would have had a hard time believing they were true at all! Now we say it is "sick" or disgusting and simply accept that such things happen. This only indicates how quickly we are moving down the slope.

But did we really get here because of a simple sabotage of language? Were we really suckered by looking to emotions for "love"?

"You can't see the forest for the trees" is an expression. And we often can't see our history for the present crises. It is hard to see how Western civilization has come to such a pass because of the glare of the Triple-X Theater and adult bookstore signs, and the teen hookers, male and female, buzzing these places like flies. We feel trapped in an endlessly sexualized culture. And if we are quiet and listen to our own minds, we can see how much we are actually caught up in that sensuality.

We see these horrors on TV but not in a way that causes us to ponder our state. We are amused, beguiled, without thought.

Where the *seed* was the emotionalization of love (as well as other virtues), that idealization was carefully cultivated and presented to Western culture. The later corruption of love to include sex signaled further confusion. Naturalism vindicated both natural emotion and natural sex drives as "healthy," and pre- or extramarital sex was on its way to acceptance, especially when done because of love or natural need.

There have been a number of periods of sexual license in Western civilization, but until this century those were clandestine and unacceptable as public policy. The Roaring Twenties was probably one of the first, fully public displays of libertine sex, but it was the sexual revolution of the sixties that finally brought the house down. This is openly acknowledged by the three feminist and sex-liberationist authors of *Re-Making Love*.[3] Even the title betrays the perverted definition of love — as the book is *entirely* about sex. In fact, this book admits that the perversion of language has continued in order to cover for the bankruptcy of "love."

> New words entered the American vocabulary: "relationship," to accommodate both marriage and "affairs" (at the same time "affair," with its permanent image of marginalization, became archaic); "lifestyle," to accommodate singleness as well as marriage (and eventually homosexuality as another "alternative").[4]

But a subtle sexualization of every facet of life was not enough. Societal pimps insisted on common exposure of the seediest, most degenerate sexual practices in the name of "openness," "honesty," and "gritty reality." The availability of such "honest" material, they argued, would help reduce sex crime by bleeding off "sexual energies." Meanwhile the rape and incest rates soared and the value of women plummeted.

The authors of *Re-Making Love* rightly point out that the sexual revolution had more impact on women's sex lives than men's.

> Put briefly, men changed their sexual behavior very little in the decades from the fifties to the eighties. They "fooled around," got married, and often fooled around some more. . . . Women, however, have gone from a pattern of virginity before marriage and monogamy thereafter to a pattern that much more resembles men.[5]

Naturally, though, the men were delighted. In fact, *Playboy* magazine has long been a supporter of sexual liberation for women, contributing money to the National Organization for Women and other women's lib groups. This way, women themselves cooperated in their own devaluation.

The authors of *Re-Making Love* clearly state that sadomasochism is the wave of the future in sex since it seems to hold out the promise of egalitarian sex (though it isn't really sex). They see nothing degrading in being tied up and whipped or vice versa. *Penthouse*, meanwhile, blazed trails further when they published pictures of a number of Asian women hanging from trees and thrown face down on jagged rocks. Asked on TV about the redeeming value of the photos, *Penthouse* editorial director, Philip Nobile said, "Oh, that's easily answered. It served the redemptive value of the artist who conceived the idea — after all, one woman's degradation is another woman's erotica."[6]

But this "liberation" was felt throughout the entire society. Nowhere was this more obvious than in the media in general and advertising in particular.

Though sex had long been used indirectly in sales during the sixties, UltraBrite toothpaste finally came out with it — "UltraBrite gives your mouth . . . sex-appeal" they crowed. Where the old commercials might show a good-looking woman standing near a new car — with all the subliminal implications, newer ads featured beautiful and often scantily clad women actually being drawn like hypnotized but voluptuous zombies toward the man behind the wheel of the sporty new car. Women in bikinis, it seemed, were irresistibly compelled to drape themselves over the hoods of certain sports cars. They also appeared interested in the tradesmen's hardware, as many were seen in photos on calendars hawking pipe wrenches and power tools.

War of the Words

The battlements of language came under heavy siege in the mid-twentieth century. This was a time when psychologists, sociologists, and others suddenly discovered that people were *sexual beings* — and they seemed to never tire of saying so. Mankind didn't seem to be "eating beings" or "sleeping beings" or "breathing beings," though considerably more time was spent doing those things, and those things were infinitely more vital to continued existence.

The endearing romantic comedies of yesteryear were the chuckles of comic misunderstanding between couples destined to marry by movie's end. Today the sex-farce, whose object is to provide a platform for filthy humor and multiple (and often kinky) bed scenes, is advertised as "romantic comedy."[7] So now, even the word *romantic* is linked to sex.

But along with these, another war of words developed: a conversion of former virtues to negative traits. *Virgin* is an excellent example of a word now said with a sneer or, at best, viewed as an obstacle to overcome. A staff writer for the *New York Times*, Anna Quindlen, reports that in a public high school restroom was the legend: *Jennifer Is a Virgin*. Quindlen says, "I asked the kids about it and they said it was shorthand for geek, nerd, weirdo, somebody who was so incredibly out of it that they were in high school and still hadn't had sex. If you were a virgin, they told me, you just lied about it."[8]

An entire genre of teen-sex movies has been devoted to young boys and girls desperately trying to free themselves from the curse of a sexless life and become "real men and women." *Pure,* as regards sex, or *chaste* would bring howls of derision. Pure, and its derivative puritanical, are, by current definition, related to "joyless," "unhappy," and judgmental of all that would give joy or happiness. Prudence, once a sought-after quality, has been shortened to "prude" and conjures up images of wiry spinsters who look as though they had been sucking persimmons.

The Meat Market

"The most unforgettable women in the world wear Revlon," reads the line below the photograph of four females dressed to resemble maenads with sultry, sexy expressions and golden flowers and leaves woven through their hair. One limpid-eyed young lady on the left appears to be about ten years old.

Sexiness is being sold here — the sexiness of a child. I think *that* is unforgettable.[9]

With the continuous bombardment of sexual images, language, and activity in the West, our imaginations and thoughts become desensitized to the pervasive sexuality of our culture. Our culture has been sold sex, and now sex is selling them. First love as emotion, then love as sex, then sex as pleasure.

In the first chapter, I described how television executives sell *us* to the advertisers. This is the first principle of advertising. But in order to sell us to them, the TV executives must sell us on our *need* for the advertised products. Thus, on TV, *all* families have dishwashers, TVs, cars, designer jeans, and other accoutrements deemed to represent normalcy. The more we accept these norms, the more we become enslaved to Madison Avenue's vision of normal life.

The media are also expert in creating *new* needs as well. Mary Pride points this out in *All The Way Home.*

Magazines do not live by subscriptions alone. They hustle for subscribers so they can turn around and sell those subscribers to advertisers. Advertising is where the big bucks are. So today magazines design their editorial content not just to please advertisers, but to help advertisers sell. The reason articles are always "continued" in another section of the magazine is so the maximum number of ads can be displayed next to the editorial content, giving the ads a better chance to be read. . . .

Advertisers, it turns out, all want a certain psychological style of reader, who could best be described as Open Mind and Open Wallet. They do not want frugal, thoughtful, hard-to-convince readers. They want readers to believe what they are told and defer their judgment to others. So editorial content ends up, by advertisers' irresistible pressure, producing dependent readers with an ever-increasing wealth of problems that need products to solve them. . . .

So magazine editorial content is strongly skewed to promoting the mentality of people who buy these things and disparaging those that don't. You don't need a more complicated explanation than that for why media writers are always campaigning *for* new fads . . . and *against* a simpler, more traditional way of life.[10]

This very same ploy has come into play in the sexual revolution as the society deteriorated into the morass of sexual habituation. As with pornography, there was an addictive quality to illicit sex, but there was also a corresponding *escalation* since last year's "new" sex rage became this year's puritanism. The sexual revolution gained momentum through the marketplace and became an amusement. Not only had Western civilization bought sex for pleasure as an axiom, but now the sexual revolution was selling the civilization to Western capitalists.

Even the proponents of the revolution readily admit this. Keeping in mind that the authors see the sexual revolution as a plus, consider the following quote.

The market for consumer goods of any kind is ever-changing, quick to absorb each new novelty [sic] and abandon the old. . . . The minute we are jaded with one product or motif, the next one arrives; and each, of course, is temporarily a necessity. . . .

Even the marketplace for sexual products both requires *and generates* [emphasis mine] variety. If sex were still what it had been in the marriage manuals of the fifties, there would be little or nothing to market. Even the now-staid and familiar vibrator would have no place in a sexual culture that denied the validity and autonomy of clitoral sexuality; flavored ointments would have no function in a culture that officially disapproved of oral sex. Sex itself had to undergo the diversification of the sexual revolution before it lent itself to being packaged and marketed in a form women could consume.

Once sexual possibilities have been "commoditized" as products and aids, the search for novelty *takes on a life of its own* [emphasis mine]. If flavored creams are exciting one year, they will be old hat the next; what is daring the first time is soon routine. So if parties like Cooper's [house parties selling sex "aids"] or stores like Pleasure Chest are to draw their customers back, something new must be found to market. It is not a sign of moral breakdown or "excessive" permissiveness that sexuality visible in the consumer culture seems to always be outreaching the old limits: This is the dynamic of the market, and in sex as well as fashion or entertainment, it pushes always and inexorably toward new frontiers.

Thus the marketplace both democratizes and *institutionalizes* the sexual revolution. . . . The perverse becomes the commonplace.[11]

Sounds like slavery to me — and blind slavery at that. The moment that you are hooked into one perversion, they begin selling you the next. Perhaps these feminist authors would think twice about the glories of the "new frontiers" pushed by the "dynamic of the market" if they saw the "fashion" ad in the liberal bastion, *The Village Voice*, which displays a drawing of a sexily clad woman lying dead on a morgue slab under the heading, "Another fashion victim."[12]

If you think that the selling of perversion has not affected you, consider the changing attitudes toward homosexuality and how it has affected laws and public life. If you are a woman, simply try to find a modest bathing suit, or look at the one you wear now and try to imagine having the courage to wear the same suit ten or twenty years ago.

Till Love Do Us Part

DEAR ALIBI: My husband (I'll call him Bob) and I have been married for four years and we have one little daughter. He has a good job and is a steady, faithful man who really goes out of his way to treat me special. I remember when we first met, how I felt about him. Bob and I just grew more and more in love all the while we dated. For the first two years of marriage, I still loved him and our sex life was fantastic. But in the last two, my feelings have changed and somehow I just don't love Bob anymore in the same way. I have also met with the man I dated before Bob (I'll call him Rick) and have discovered I still love him. I am thinking of leaving Bob and going with Rick, but I know how much that would upset Bob and both our families. Still, I feel unfulfilled without Rick. What should I do? — Confused in Freedonia

DEAR CONFUSED: Indeed it may be difficult for Bob and the families, but if they are mature, non-judgmental people they will realize that you must do what is right for you. You are the only one who can judge your own feelings. You just have to go with your feelings.

ᔰ   ᔰ   ᔰ

I admit that most columnists would not give such advice straight out, but this *is* the message of our culture. Over and over we hear it: Go with your feelings. Get in touch with your own feelings. Do what's right for you. Only you know your feelings.

So, is it a surprise that marriage is an endangered institution, that women file for more divorces than men? Even before the sexual revolution most people were convinced that marriage was something you did with another when you had a certain *feeling* about one another. That feeling, however, was impossible to define. Thus the endless discussions on the difference between "true love" and "puppy love" or infatuation. There was constant worry over whether "it" was "the real thing" or not—thus also the perennial conversation, "Dad, how will I know when I'm *really* in love?" "You'll know, my son. You'll just know." These epitomize the confusion created by the redefinition of love. Western culture and its lore is literally saturated with the goopy stuff. Think of all the horror tales of beautiful young women being callously doled out to cruel, old, ugly misers by unfeeling fathers.

Now, social conventions against divorce stood for a long time, but many a "love" story was predicated on adultery justified by "love." And if adultery could be so justified, it soon became apparent that divorce could as well. Once the West was sold on the idea of marriage based on love—and arranged marriages all but ceased—then it was no stretch to dissolve marriage based on lack of love. Now, as people slip in and out of marriages like so many changes of clothing, they tell us, "The marriage just didn't work," as though it were the marriage that was supposed to do the work. Others pass off the whole thing as a "growth experience"—one that leaves broken children behind.

But some brave souls out there are even dropping the pretense of love—a trend best illustrated by a bumper sticker I saw on a car with a good-looking young couple in it: "Forget love; Go for lust!"

This attitude is the direct consequence of believing that the purpose of sex is pleasure. This precept came out of naturalistic science and was regarded, for many years, as the sole property of the male. But when Margaret Sanger began bawling for her rights to enjoy sex, the men were pleased as punch. To them, if women were thus liberated, it just increased the supply of women available to them. If the ladies *wanted* to jump into the swill . . . well, the more the merrier. The immediate barrier to this idea were those nasty little surprises—babies. But since the thirties when the first Christian denomination broke ranks in opposition to artificial birth control, much "progress" was made to include all women in the ranks of sex-charged hedonists.

After the leak sprung in church opposition, it was not long before the idea of birth control took hold nationally. But the idea that one could choose when—or if—to have children implied a right to pleasure without responsibility. Since sex was already accepted as a right, it was only a hop-skip-and-a-jump to eliminate the consequences. The right to control fertility implied, and eventually secured, the right to abortion.

All this was building until the sixties when the natural conclusions of these beliefs came home to roost. If marriage was for love, why have marriage? People could love without it, couldn't they? Couples who were shacking up whined, "Why do we need a piece of paper to prove that we love each other?" as they bounced from one bedroom to another. Sociologists touted the *trial marriage* where the couple took each other out for a test sex drive for several months or years before committing it to paper. The pseudo-scientists intoned that this would strengthen the marriages that resulted. Later studies were to disprove the theory, but even that did not discourage the ever-optimistic "scientists" who excused the faltering hypothesis, stating the obvious, "In a sense, the meaning of marriage may be different for people who cohabit and then marry than for those who marry."[13]

Other studies conclusively showed that women who started sex at early ages and had many partners were many times more likely to develop serious cervical cancers. These could end any possibilities of having children or even kill. But the medical community blithely responded that it was not necessary for anyone to change their lifestyle, but they should come in for more frequent checkups.[14]

When casual sex began to ring up charges of the gift that keeps on giving — herpes — and the gift that is forever — AIDS — everyone was advised to "be more careful about your partners." Doctors and counselors said, "Only have sex with someone you *really* know." They said, "Practice 'safe' sex." But sex was a constitutional right, and they would defend it to their deaths in the AIDS wards.

So, love, which had been the reason for marriage, soon became the reason for not marrying. Sex, which existed for pleasure, could be found anywhere — marriage was an anachronism.

Androgyny and Autonomy

It was only natural that once sex was entirely equated with pleasure that someone would suggest that, all things being equal, it didn't matter who (or what) one had sex with, so long as it was personally satisfying and fulfilling. Sex had become primarily self-gratifying. In fact, feminist writer Betty Friedan called heterosexual intercourse "vaginal masturbation" for the men. But the sexual revolution changed all that. Sex between partners (hetero-, homo-, or group) was now *mutual* masturbation. Really, it didn't matter if you had sex with your shoe.

In the early seventies, books were written extolling masturbation. One was titled, *Sex for One: The Joy of Self-Loving (Illustrated).*[15] Again we see the perverse definition of love as sex. Most self-love proponents, even today, would be aghast at this distortion. Yet, it is the logical sequel to the self-love doctrine. Recalling what the author of this bizarre tome means by self-love, the dedication was revealing: "This book is dedicated to me. Without my self-love it would never have been written." That sounds like someone with terrific "self-esteem," not to mention self-love.

Of course, the homosexual movement took off as well. Who, after all, could deny their *feelings?* Why should others be offended by who they loved? The homosexuals and others were beginning to identify their entire existence on the narrow basis of their preferences in sex. Each person was autonomous and androgynous. Sexual activities were for them, by them, and about them—whether they chose opposite sex, same sex, self sex, or some other sex. It was a mockery of the unity in married sex. These people were trying to become one, all right—one with themselves.

Women's World

Women, once the compelling force behind home, family, and morality, were now so busy trying to "find themselves" that everything was left behind. Their high calling in childbearing, child-nurturing, nursing, and homemaking denied, they began to artificially pursue the worst male attributes. The newly minted value system (i.e., everything's value could be measured in terms of sex or sexiness) captured their attention, and they began to market themselves by their sexual features. Women's magazines greased the skids trumpeting, "Just say yes to sexy." Clearly the message was, "You're in this for your own pleasure, so go for it!"

Women were labeling themselves as "sex objects." The brave and bold among them shrieked at male stripper shows (as they imagined men do with female strippers), bought and used sex toys, or joined swinger groups. The timorous went on their escapades through the fantasy life of women's porn: the romance novels and soap operas, which they insisted mirror "real life."

A Skin Trade in Children

Screams shattered the peaceful night of the suburban Carmichael, California — children's screams. Neighbors notified police. A schoolteacher recognized the distress in the piercing sounds. "It was much too high-pitched and intense to be nightmares," she said. "Kids don't have nightmares like that night after night."

But police found no hard evidence of abuse by the divorced father of the children and soon, they left.

Later investigation, however, resulted in charges being filed against the father who had been selling his daughters, four-years-old and ten-years-old, for $55 to $85 to molesters. Dad took pictures and sold them as well.[16]

             a   *a*   *a*

The magazines are heaped upon the coffee table in the middle-class suburban home. It is the faces that first catch your attention — young faces — eight-, ten-, twelve-year-olds — boys and girls. The titles deliver one jolt after another: *Lolitots, Life-Boy, Moppets, Torrid Tots, Perverse Lolitas, Bambina Sex.*

It seems unbelievable. How did this happen? How was a market for this swill generated? How did *children* get sold into sexual slavery?

We are appalled at the idea. We cringe and choke at the thought of the real children behind those deeply haunted faces on *Goldenboys* and *Schoolgirls*. Yet, we seem to be blind to the pervasive pimping of our own children in Western society which might prepare tender minds for such a fate.

Advertisers often show children leering sensually at one another. Kiddie makeup kits are hawked as glamour items to eight-year-olds. Now a child in a bikini has invaded the sultry European-style sexuality of the well-established Bain de Soleil suntan lotion ads. One menswear ad showed a shirtless man standing with a nightgowned little girl in the gauze draped background.

Another little girl is shown sitting with one knee up, her skirt sliding up giving a lurid show of her thigh. A chain was draped across her leg — the sadomasochistic implications were subtle but clear.[17] A new Hollywood favorite is to spew forth vile profanities and sexual double entendres from a sweet-faced child.[18]

Daily we sell our children to the skin trade of sex education in public schools, which has been shown to merely increase the level of tolerance for perverse sex[19] while having virtually no effect on child pregnancy except to increase it. AIDS education is now being used to introduce grade-schoolers to the distorted sex of homosexuals.

Across the nation, public school teachers are showing violent, pornographic films to high school students under the guise of "academic freedom." Some of these are suing balking school principals and school districts for these "rights."[20]

Add to this the the statistic that 70 percent of all pornographic magazines end up in the hands of children. In the early eighties, there was a rash of teen deaths attributed to suicide — deaths which were, in actuality, caused by failed attempts at a fashionable brand of "auto-eroticism" (masturbation) which involved a sexual climax while asphyxiation was setting in. This gruesome practice was touted in *Hustler* and other pornographic magazines as an ultimate sexual experience. A number of young men died trying to find out.[21] In some cases the magazines were still in their laps opened to the article which detailed the process.

Imagine how driven — how enslaved to the sexual culture — a young man would have to be to risk death itself for an ecstatic sexual experience. The truth was so awful that parents, police, and press felt compelled to call them suicides rather than death by sexual slavery.

The Role of TV and Music

One survey shows that the top two pressures on the young to become involved in sex are TV and music. Show after show on television presents sex for teens as the norm. Parents on programs like *Kate and Allie, My Two Dads,* and *Heartbeat* will be initially upset about their child "becoming sexually active," but the local VOR (Voice Of Reason) will prevail and convince Dad to understand. Many of the children are told that their heart will tell them if it is time to begin having sex.

Aristotle said, "Music has the power to form character." And it appears to be so. What behavior can we expect to result from repeated listenings to music artists whose message is that sex is good anytime, anywhere, and with anyone?

In one song alone, rock superstar Prince uses the F-word seventeen times. His ten-million-seller album, *Purple Rain,* included the lyrics, "I knew a girl named Nikki / I guess you would say she was a sex fiend / I met her in a hotel lobby masturbating with a magazine. . . ." Nor does Prince shy away from incest. In his song *Sister,* on another album, he sings, "My sister never made love to anyone else but me / Incest is everything it's said to be." Tina Turner explains to the kids that sex is only for pleasure when she sings in *What's Love Got To Do With It,* "It's only physical / You must ignore that it means more than that / What's love but a secondhand emotion?"[22]

And we blather on about when teens become sexually active as though it were the inevitable sprouting of a new tooth. One morning they wake to find themselves "sexually active," and there's nothing that can be done about it.

The Push for Sexual Liberation of Children

The respectable seeming Planned Parenthood has returned to the sexual liberationist roots of its nymphomaniac founder Margaret Sanger and has launched an all out campaign to sexually liberate the young.

"No religious views, no moral standards, are to deflect the child from overriding purposes of self-discovery, self-assertion, and self-gratification,"[23] thundered one PP luminary. Not to be outdone, Rocky Mountain Planned Parenthood published *The Perils of Puberty* and intoned, "Sex is too important to glop it up with sentiment. If you feel sexy, for heaven's sake, admit it to yourself. If the feeling and the tension bother you, you can masturbate."

But Planned Parenthood was not satisfied with targeting only those entering puberty. It was *children* that they wanted most to "liberate." One PP representative, Wardell B. Pomeroy, posited, "Incest between adults and younger children can also prove to be a satisfying and enriching experience. Incestuous relationships can — and do — work out well."[24]

In March of 1974, *Ms. Magazine,* then edited by Gloria Steinem, printed "A Child's Bill of Rights." Number 7 of the list is as follows:

> The Right to Sexual Freedom. *Children have the right to conduct their sexual lives with no more restriction than adults.* Sexual freedom for children must include the right to information about sex, the right to nonsexist education, and the right to all sexual activities that are legal among consenting adults.[25] (Emphasis in the original)

The concern of society for the degradation of youth was clearly reflected when U.S. District Judge Alan McDonald suspended a five-year sentence for convicted child pornographer, Howard Dean Johnson. The judge only had the Kittitas, Washington, city employee serve thirty days and perform two hundred hours of community service.

In another case, Hamilton County, Ohio Judge Gilbert Bettman sentenced R. Terrence Ormond to four months and a five-hundred-dollar fine. Ormond posed as a psychologist and author to lure four girls, ages ten through twelve, into his home where he showed them pornography and sexually molested them. Judge Bettman had formerly gained local notoriety for sentencing one who had raped a nine-year-old to ninety days. Bettman claimed that he had reduced the sentence because the nine-year-old had given her consent.[26] That a nine-year-old would be deemed *capable* of such consent reveals the extent to which we expect children to be sexually sophisticated.

In 1985, in Holland, the legislature seriously considered a bill to lower the age of consent for sex from sixteen to twelve years of age.[27] The bill did not pass, but it was seriously debated.

Annually, participants march down the streets of New York City in the Gay Pride Parade along with the National Man/Boy Love Association which advocates total abolition of all age of consent laws for sex between adults and children.

Here, at childhood, meet the distortion of love and the perversion of sex. Just as with the three previous chapters on pornography, prostitution, and homosexuality, the perversion trail ends with the destruction of innocence — the perversion of childhood.

What We Have Seen

- The perversion of love as emotion and sex finally broke into a run in the sexual revolution of the 1960s.

- Twisted terms, such as *lifestyle* and *relationship,* were added to the common speech to fuel the fires of degeneration.

- Terms describing virtue were ridiculed and denigrated.

- Being out of "love" became sufficient cause for divorce.

- Divorce skyrocketed.

- Women abandoned their position as stabilizers of family and society and plunged into *free sex.*

- Advertisers and media began to sexualize every message.

- Advertisers soon were selling illicit sex as much as products.

- Illicit sex requires escalation in order to continue to satisfy.

- By this stage, even when free sex began to prove to be very expensive, the society was unwilling to deny itself the pleasure, so it denied the evidence.

- Sex viewed as pleasure led to the rapid movement toward sexual anarchy expressed in the glorification of masturbation, homosexuality, and sadomasochism.

- The culture was blinded to distinctions of age and began to prey on its own children and use them as sex objects.

What We Will See

We will look at the church's response to the siren call of sexual liberation. We will see that, by and large, the church has been mesmerized by the twin doctrines of "marriage for love" and "sex for pleasure." Because of the acceptance of these heresies, Christians have had little ground to stand on in defending absolute sexual purity. Consequently, more and more compromises were made in bowing to the god of "reality."

These compromises are proving to be a fatal weakness as more leading Christian teachers defect and justify unbiblical sexual behavior.

Since the church of Jesus Christ is "the pillar and ground of the truth," if it fails there will be nothing between Western civilization and the ignominious destruction which has buried all previous perverted regimes.

9

THE CHURCH SLIPS:
A DART IN THE LIVER

The man was at the very edge of the cliff. He was walking the extremity of the sheer precipice — backwards. Just as he lifted his front foot, the gusty wind increased and he swayed back and forth, nearly pitching himself headlong to the boulders fifty yards below.

Regaining his steadiness, he placed the foot down behind him exactly parallel to the line of the edge. Half the footing suddenly crumbled and fell until it disappeared from sight below. Again, he steadied himself.

Then he raised his front foot . . .

ra   ra   ra

The Western churchman stands on the precipice and says, "Will I get in trouble with God if I . . . use the company copier machine for my stuff?"

"What if I use the company car to run an errand for my wife (he raises his right foot)? Or maybe a little

167

gas in my car on the company card?" he asks (as the gust of wind threatens to pitch him over the edge).

"After all, it is *practically* company policy," he says (struggling to regain his balance). "Well, I guess not (he steadies himself)."

"But I do need to run that errand," he says (placing the foot behind himself). "And maybe I should stop and get a haircut while I'm at it (the edge crumbles)."

"Should probably count that as my lunch time," he cautions himself (steadying again).

ès   ès   ès

To the modern Christian in the West the question is not, "How can I get closer to God?" but the cynical, "How much can I get away with without actually sinning?"

"I can smoke (or not attend church, miss prayer and Bible reading, have a beer, read an article in *Playboy*) and still be a Christian," seems to be the prevailing attitude. And maybe you *can* do some of those things, but why do we seem to always try to stake out the outer limits of God's grace. There is almost a desperate urge to show how "free" we are by daring the edges of enslaving sin. I call this urge *the carnal nature.* Feeding this carnal urge is the false idea that it is *the ability to sin* which defines freedom, and *not* the ability *not* to sin. In *How to Say NO to a Stubborn Habit,* Erwin W. Lutzer analyzes this problem like this:

> Perhaps you are now beginning to understand why
> you cannot begin to break your sinful habit unless

you believe in God's goodness. The reason is simple: if you doubt God's goodness you will not want to change. You'll be convinced that God wants to rob you rather than enrich you.

I've discovered that the most frustrating problem in helping those who come for counsel is simply that most people do not want to change. Of course, they are prepared to make minor adjustments — particularly if their behavior is getting them into trouble. But most of them are comfortable with their sin as long as it doesn't get out of hand. And they'd prefer to have God keep His activity in their lives to a minimum.[1]

This cogent observation is reminiscent of the Scripture's statement that men love darkness rather than light because their deeds are evil (see John 3:19).

But another root of such spiritual gerrymandering was illustrated at the beginning of this book where virtues (real qualities attainable from God) were changed to ideals (unreachable goals partially experienced by feelings). This became true of love, compassion, bravery, loyalty, and all the others. It was not long before Christians believed that they could not hope to attain the ideals reached by a select few; they would have to settle for occasional flashes of compassionate feelings — or feelings of holiness. Christians had lost that keen sense of striving for holiness.

Again, I will ask: Am I saying that emotions or feelings are sin? *No!* I am saying that the *feeling* of love (or other virtues) cannot be used to supplant the actual performance of loving deeds.

The idea that such virtues as courage actually existed and were attainable was proven by the stories of the multitudes of martyrs during the first several centuries of the church. Their courage was more than a feeling. But soon they too were safely idealized and isolated from common reality.

If ideals could not be reached, then it was only reasonable to carve out territories that were regarded as "acceptable levels of righteousness." This, viewed from God's perspective, was more like allotting an acceptable level of sin (a Protestant version of indulgences). Churches sprang up whose only difference between them and their "mother" churches was their "acceptable level of righteousness" (whether higher or lower). This kind of thing was actually the major fault of the Pharisees of Jesus' time. It wasn't so much that they were actually righteous according to the law — or even trying to be — but that they found their own "acceptable level of righteousness" and despised those who did not follow suit.

Today, when a Christian seriously strives for perfection, other churchmen do not encourage him but rather slander him as self-righteous or pharisaical. Mediocrity is even too high a standard as many churches virtually trample one another in the dash to become "relevant" to all members. What they actually mean is to lower the standard until *anyone* can meet it — the

World War II "convoy method" of moving at the speed of the slowest ship.

Terms of Surrender[2]

For the most part, the modern church has accepted the love-as-emotion doctrine for centuries. The *mainline* denominations began their rapid descent in the earlier decades of this century. Fundamental and evangelical groups were more tenacious, but the grip began to slip in the fifties and sixties. There was still, however, a commitment to morality that forbade unbridled emotionalism. But though mainline denominations often protest, their usage of the word *love* betrays their dependence on the Love Myth. This is even more profound today. Consider the words to many of the recent Christian songs, especially in the ranks of *contemporary* Christian music. Note the parallel with other contemporary music in its emphasis on "how Jesus makes *me* feel." Like modern love songs, love is a *feeling* of the singer, not a *commitment* to the one loved.

To see the real impact of the earlier century's capitulation, we must examine the 1960s. This was a time when the West was literally flooded with a *love* revolution that catastrophically changed the culture. In the midst of the most materialistic times (coming out of the fifties), Western civilization was hit by a wave that overturned most moral conventions — deeming them archaic — and left people tossed in a sea of uncertainty. "Love is all you need," was the message. And *love* was good feelings, good times, niceness, world peace, and sex — *certainly* sex. People who "loved" each other obviously had sex — how else would they express it? Satan had a field day sabotaging language, and the drug-soaked minds ate it up.

Now what these young druggies believed would have been all for naught had it not been for the two fellow-travelers, Hollywood and Madison Avenue, who smelled money in the whole thing. Soon hippiedom's psychedelic products and movies were vomiting out of "establishment" businesses. These parent-supported young people were soon plastering stickers and posters everywhere, panhandling to buy albums and concert tickets. But beyond that, Madison Avenue saw these kids as the consumers of the future and began gearing commercials with "love" messages, sex messages, *feeling* messages. In this way they also carried the love-as-feeling-and-sex message to the general public and began the brainwash bombardment.

Upon this mystically steeped generation came a mighty sweep of the Holy Spirit and, like the dragnet of the parable (see Matthew 13:47-50), caught fish both good and bad. The church, as usual, was caught unprepared but soon began opening outreaches for the strange street urchins. Of course, in the minds of the hippies, they had always followed "love" and peace, which was what was commanded in the Bible, "Love one another," right?

The leaders of the unready church outreaches did not wish to drive away these young people, so many of them did not immediately quibble over the definitions of *love* and *peace*. The problem was, no one ever got around to clearing up the conflicting definitions.

Many of the Jesus People felt called to ministry and went on to seminaries. Even here the distorted terminology was not confronted. Today, many of these same people inhabit church pulpits, boards, seminary posts, and even the writing-and-lecture circuit. All of this with much of the emotional baggage from their sixties experience.

Am I overemphasizing the power of definition? I don't think so. Proverbs tells us that "He who is perverted [twisted] in his language falls into evil."[3] One example of the confusion of the Love Myth with the fruit of the Spirit is found in a popular Christian sex manual:

> Love is an *emotion* that must be cultivated; *no Christian should endure marriage without it.* The first characteristic of the Spirit-filled life is love.[4] (Emphasis added)

Another serious consequence of the devaluation of love was the forced extinction of the fear of the Lord. It soon became popular to wag a finger at anyone who brought it up saying, "Well, you know, brother, 'perfect love casts out all fear.'" This scriptural distortion was only possible because the church succumbed to the Love Myth.

Purity in the Church

Many of us remember the ad: Ivory soap is $99^{44}/_{100}$ percent pure. The phrase has taken up permanent residence in the American idiom and is still on Ivory's label.

I am not referring to the soap, however, when I say, "$99^{44}/_{100}$ percent isn't pure enough — when it comes to God." Yet $99^{44}/_{100}$ percent pure is the way Western Christians tend to view their faith. Perhaps they've never asked themselves the question, "Pure what?"[5] For if it is pure sewage, it would not be particularly pertinent that it was pure. Even assuming that the $99^{44}/_{100}$ percent pure is referring to what actually is pure, what is the remaining $^{56}/_{100}$ percent? In a $99^{44}/_{100}$ percent pure apple, the remainder could be strychnine; in water, the fraction could be sewage.

All this is meant to illustrate what was written in the Song of Solomon, that it is the little foxes that spoil the vine (2:15). The church acceptance of love as an emotion has stripped it of vital defenses. While some people contend that we should not debate over words, I beg to remind them how much the Scripture has to say about perverse or twisted speech. It may seem petty to quibble over definitions but, for example, 1½ million babies are slaughtered every year in America over the definition of the word *choice*.

And, to God, purity *is* important — and *commanded*, not suggested.

Counting the Cost of Compromise

It began when Sam was in fourth grade. In a dusty nook in a corner of an old Army barracks he found the pictures. Sam knew they were wrong, yet he was strangely drawn to them. There were lots of corners in the creaky temporary housing to hide the pornography, and Sam used them all. Day after day, he went back — until he was caught.

But the fascination never left him. Over the years, pornography was hard to come by, but Sam always seemed to find just enough. It was when he entered high school that he began to realize it was out of control. It felt like another being was inside driving him on for more of the filthy stuff. Even Sam's heavy involvement in church work, campus ministry, his prayers, and his strivings only seemed to be masks as he went on to deeper depravity. The conflict and contradiction tore at his soul as he slinked to his room to masturbate over lurid photos. Even his sister catching him once only briefly dampened the drive.

After about three years in high school, Sam was able to summon the courage to face some of the other leaders of the Christian club of which he was president and share the secret with them.

"I finally knew I wasn't alone," Sam says as he recalls that others among them were struggling with similar problems. "I knew I wasn't some kind of freak." His torment yielded for about a month. But soon the overpowering urges consumed him again, blinding him to even the possible consequences of public disclosure.

Yet with the encouragement of his peers' acceptance, Sam sought help from his parents. His mother wept and prayed with him, but his father was uncomprehending. Once again the cramping straps of bondage loosened. But even this relief was short-lived.

Driven by utter despair and deep desperation, Sam called his pastor for an appointment.

So on a warm summer afternoon he walked the rural town road toward the brick church. The tension inside tempted him to forego the upcoming confession, but Sam *really* wanted help. The appointed time with his pastor rapidly approached. As he walked up to the office door he caught the smell of new-mowed grass and heard the deep thrumming of the power mower in the yard next to the church. Sam was apprehensive about how to begin the delicate conversation, but there was a deep-seated confidence that now — finally — something would be done about this demonic slavery.

It was cool as Sam entered the pastor's study. Two sides of the room were walled with books; pastor was a very well educated man. At the desk on the left the balding man half rose and greeted Sam. Sam knew the pastor well and was quite comfortable with him.

"I wanted to talk to you about something I recently shared with a couple of friends," Sam began tentatively. Then he laid out the problem — compulsive use of pornography and masturbation. Sam saw no sign of shock on the pastor's face.

The response came almost as reflex. Pastor explained that he, too, had sexual struggles. "You'll grow out of it," he told Sam regarding masturbation. By the end of the dizzying conversation it seemed that the only problem the pastor could see was the dependency on pornography, but he offered no solution.

Bitterly disappointed, Sam left the church office. He thought over the years he had slowly been sucked into bondage — all those years while he was still faithfully attending church. "Why had there never been a warning — a warning from the pulpit? from the Sunday school? from someplace?"

Now even his long struggle to cry for help had been treated as a teenage phase.

It was ten more years to deliverance at the hand of God.[6]

     🙠   🙠   🙠

In this story the church failed a desperate teen trapped in a sinful web. How did it happen? The pastor had come, like many, to believe that it was impossible for young men to entirely control their sex urges — that the *feelings* were simply too strong. So, this pastor settled on his own "acceptable level of righteousness" for teens. Sexually, he decided, teens need only be 99 $^{44}/_{100}$ percent pure.

These compromises had been long in coming and, in many cases, were simply a pervasive belief that was not often committed to writing. But the idea that masturbation was not necessarily wrong gained ascendancy and was to prove to be the crack in the dike.

Seminary professors began to parrot. the liberal church line that masturbation was not mentioned in the Bible. They skillfully excised self-abuse from the Greek catch-all word for sex outside of marriage — *porneia.*

Even the story of Onan (see Genesis 38:8) was converted into a tale of disobedience to the Law of Moses — a law that was four hundred years from being written. Understanding Onan's sin as masturbation was branded as a peculiar Roman Catholic teaching unworthy of enlightened Protestants. The fact is that in Onan's time the Levirate duty to raise seed for one's brother was a local custom. It was for violation of this that modernist theologians say that Onan died. Yet, if this were so, God should also have killed Onan's brother, Shelah, and his father, Jacob. Even more, God would certainly have made this violation a death penalty offense in Moses' law. Instead, such violators were spat upon and called a derisive name — hardly a comparable punishment to that suffered by Onan. Obviously, more was involved than simply the failure to fulfill the Levirate duty.[7]

The real reason, however, that many could not accept the prohibition against masturbation was simply that it was *old.* It wasn't *modern* to think like that. After all, naturalistic science had "proved" that young men needed such release. It was only an "old superstition" or a "cultural prejudice" that caused the early church to prohibit a natural release of sexual tensions. But despite the fact that some early Christians had died rather than violate such "cultural prejudices," *modern* Christians appeared to feel that studying *why* they felt that way was a waste of time. It was *old*, that was enough to condemn it. The more Biblically minded also skipped the research and labeled such things as "traditions of men."

The more conservative Christians warned that it should not become habitual (though they could scarcely give a clear line there — once a week? three times a day?) and that it should not be accompanied by "lustful thoughts" — as though masturbation were possible without it. This sprung open the door.

Knowing that books giving permission to sin would sell, the Christian publishing industry cranked up the presses. One publisher was reported as having said of the books that sell best, that they impart "Biblical optimism that encourages people in the normal paths of life, integrating Biblical truth into today's journey and today's lifestyle." He later spoke of the great need for books that "scratch people where they itch."[8]

One recent book on marriage and sex was *Christians in the Wake of the Sexual Revolution.*[9] This otherwise fine book was a clearly stated prohibition of all illicit sex and lust — until the author came upon the masturbation question. Here he committed a serious blunder by not linking it to such obvious passages as "flee youthful lusts" and "flee fornication" (1 Timothy 2:22; 1 Corinthians 6:18). Neither of these admonitions leaves much room for discussion — or even examination — of the issue. This book slams the door on premarital sex, only to open it a crack and leave it ajar. While the author says that nearly all masturbation is accompanied by lust and is therefore prohibited, there is still enough room left for human nature to justify itself. Though this was hardly the author's intention, this is precisely the kind of wedge that eventually will be used to loosen the remaining moral boundaries. The whole controversy seems to revolve around an abandonment of God's stated purpose for marriage and sex. With God the issue is sex itself, not just lust.

But the above author is not alone. Many well known Christian leaders cannot seem to find masturbation in Scripture (which, I might add, is also true of a whole range of sexual practices of homosexuals and perverts: sadomasochism, oral and anal sex, fisting, shoe fettishes, etc.). Again, in their minds, the word *fornication* doesn't seem to apply.

The Rev. Tim and Mrs. Beverly LaHaye appear to have some essential grasp on why masturbation is wrong.[10] *Their* fatal error on the matter, like so many others, lay in their words, "Unfortunately the Bible is silent on the subject. . . ." To me, this clearly indicates the isolation of the Western church from early Biblical understandings.

But it doesn't stop there. Another well-known speaker on the subject called masturbation, "God's gift to the single person."[11]

The reason for my seriousness about this issue is simply that the Bible plainly states that "no fornicator will enter the Kingdom of God" (1 Corinthians 6:9-10). If masturbation has even the slightest chance of being included as fornication, think of the effects on the young people reading such advice. Think of mill-stones! Remember the man on the cliff's edge.

Flights of Fantasy

Sexual temptations in many forms have always lured Christians, but today's climate seems to offer more opportunities than past history. One report has it that a recent convention of youth pastors created the highest rental of X-rated movies in the hotel's history.[12]

As we have noted before, fantasy plays an essential role in both sales and seduction. This has been true in the seduction of the Western church. In recent decades, the skin trade has been made to look appealing. Sexuality has been flaunted in a way that enticed Christians to imagine how much fun it must be to be involved in illicit sex.

Now the Bible acknowledges quite openly that sin can be fun, but warns that its wages are not (see Romans 6:23). But the mentality of Western Christians was to value freedom and measure freedom by how much they could "get away with" rather than how much they could get away *from.* Those formerly enslaved to sin began judging their freedom by how close to sin they could stay. The proverb comes to mind: "As a dog returneth to his vomit, so a fool returneth to his folly" (Proverbs 26:11).

In skirting the precipice of sin, many fell, some were sorely injured, others died. But it was the *fantasy* that sin was fun, bold, and free that started them coming in droves.

The feminist, sexual liberationist authors of *Re-Making Love* gloat over the sexual revolution's influence on the Christian community. In a chapter entitled, "Fundamentalist Sex: Hitting Below the Bible Belt," they chortle, "But the biggest and best prize [for Christian women] was a new sex life. In *Total Joy,* (Marabel) Morgan sounded as if she'd read either *The Sensuous Woman* or *Our Bodies, Ourselves,* both banned in Christian bookstores."[13]

So, while the church memorized Bible verses like, "Do not be conformed to this world . . . "[14] they were also reading about the joy of Christian sex and lapping up sanctified versions of the secular sexual revolution's offerings.

Morgan and her *Total Woman* book and seminars tapped into the fantasy market by recommending that wives meet their husbands at the door in costume: a miniskirted cowgirl, a spy with nothing under the trenchcoat, a stripper. All this may temporarily add excitement to the sex life (as though that were its *purpose*) but it is also very dangerous. Morgan's method actually used taboos as a spice. But after all the costumes had been used — what then? The wife had succeeded in tantalizing her husband with *fantasy* — perhaps to imagine himself with *other* women (a clear violation of Jesus' words about lusting after other women, see Matthew 5:28). The authors of *Re-*

Making Love point to the origins and the intents of the *Total Woman* format.

> Morgan, *operating out of the newly changed mores of the sixties and seventies,* tried to turn the forbidden into something "as pure as cottage cheese," but with a little spice added. "Costumes provide variety without him ever leaving home," she wrote, promising men (and women) *the same exotic thrill a secret affair might give.*[15] (Emphasis added)

The woman who takes this advice is tapping into the thought life of the ever-ready and dangerous carnal nature — the carnal desire for *illicit* sex. It is difficult enough to corral *unwanted* fantasy without having it deliberately stimulated by one's wife.

Remember also that illicit sex tends to escalate. So unless the wife is willing to progress from dress-up, to using pornography, to sadomasochism, to wife swapping, or any other side trail, she should abandon this dangerous tactic. This process is known as the *law of diminishing returns* and is particularly rapid in illicit sex. Improving the sex life is simply not an ultimate value; it is not worth the cost.

The idea is not that someone cannot dress as a cowgirl, but what is the impulse in the man that she is going to arouse? Why must we always be in jeopardy of being pitched "onto the boulders fifty yards below?"

Any competent Christian minister can vouch for the huge increase in sexual problems among Christians since the church began to validate the "Christian sex manual" approach. Naturally, there are cries from some quarters that these problems *always* existed and are only now coming to light. While it may be true that recent decades had submerged problems which were precursors to the present deluge, I don't seem to recall Peter, Paul, and James being inundated with counseling requests from those with "sexual difficulties" or those considering divorce (and converts often came out of *extreme* sexual licentiousness). Skyrocketing divorce rates among even evangelical Christians testify to the deterioration.

The total woman who feeds her husband's carnal desire for taboo sex may easily end up as the *totaled* woman.

The success, however, of the *Total Woman* courses was enormous within the American church. Even her more conservative detractors have since been edged toward further sexual "liberation." The influence and infiltration of the secular version of the liberation into the Western church is easily documented and openly crowed by the perversion pushers. The name of the church, its doctrines, and even Christ Himself is mocked.[16]

The Pleasure Principle — Christian Style

Somebody finally said it. "Sex is fun," they said in a teen class on sex — *in church!* This was treated as a real breakthrough in the sixties for the church to openly state the obvious. "Why had the church been silent so long?" some seemed to ask.

Perhaps it was that there were more important issues to concern them—like sexual purity, like fleeing fornication, like holiness. But even with these, the church seemed to lack solid argument. Why, for instance, should someone stay sexually pure or flee fornication? Part of the trouble lay in the fact that most of the Western church had no ground left to stand on. It had cast aside the teachings of Scripture on the purpose for marriage and sex. It tried to stand primarily on naturalistic science in its prohibition of sex outside of marriage. In essence, the church left the rock for the sand.

Soon its primary teaching against premarital sex consisted of warnings against pregnancy and venereal diseases. It also threw in some more dubious warnings about physiological and psychological problems that certain experts guessed might befall the unwary sexual experimenter.

There were several problems with this approach: (1) God uses none of these arguments. His objection is that the sex act itself is sacred and reserved for marriage. Period. (2) The threats of pregnancy and venereal disease have (at this time) been greatly reduced by "our friend, Mr. Science."

The church was left with foundering arguments.

But the sex-is-fun theologians didn't stop with teen groups. Due to the massive bombardment of the devolving culture, the pleasure principle had become the *focus* of the issue—in the secular arena, years before;

now, in the church. The *Total Woman* philosophy of
Marabel Morgan had put a high profile on sexual satisfaction and pleasure. Birth control, now gaining
church-wide acceptance as a "tool for stewardship,"
had divorced sex from childbearing. Christians, rabidly
searching for "meaning" in sex (after having abandoned God's), picked up on pleasure as the "meaning"
of sex. But it was almost impossible for them to be so
crass as to say it outright, so most contrived to connect
the pleasure of sex with the unity or "one flesh" aspects. The word *intimacy* was frequently tapped to
sanctify a consuming interest in pleasure.

One of the landmark Christian sex manuals was
written by Dr. Ed Wheat and his wife, Gaye. The title
itself indicates that the *purpose* of sex had become pleasure — *Intended for Pleasure: New Approaches to Sexual
Intimacy in Christian Marriage.* Here the confusion between the principle of unity and the pleasure principle
hit a profound note. The Wheats' interpretation of 1 Corinthians 7:3-5 is stunning in its implications.

> God's viewpoint comes forth vigorously in 1 Corin-
> thians 7:3-5 where the husband and wife are told
> they actually *defraud* [emphasis theirs] one another
> when they refuse to give physical pleasure and satis-
> faction to their mate.[17]

But they do not stop at this. They place sexual satisfaction in the category of a *right* and that it is *mutual
sexual satisfaction,* not simple unity in the marriage

act, that qualifies as the demonstration of the unity of Christ and the church.

> God says husband and wife have the right to be sexually satisfied.[18]

> Ephesians 5:31, 32 spells it out: "For this cause shall a man leave his father and mother, and shall be joined unto his wife, and the two shall become one flesh. This is a great mystery, but I speak concerning Christ and the church." *Thus, the properly and lovingly executed and mutually satisfying sexual union is God's way of demonstrating to us a great spiritual truth.* (italics in the original)[19]

Evidently, the clumsily executed, hurried, or blandly unsatisfying encounters do not allow the two to become one flesh and do not represent an allegory of Christ and the church. Newlyweds could escape "becoming one" for quite some time — especially if they had abstained from sex before marriage. People who had been unfortunate enough to be raised unliberated and did not focus on the pleasure of sex at all, could possibly miss the kingdom entirely. But then, the other spouse (not so inhibited) would be missing his or her "rights" to sexual satisfaction.

Am I being too caustic? The implications are all there in the Wheats' text (bolstered by comments from other Christian sex manuals).[20] If *they* purpose to crassly connect the beautiful imagery of unity between Christ and the church with sexual *pleasure,* then I hardly think my extrapolation can be contradicted. In fact, it is *they* who commend masturbation when coital sex is unavailable, for example, during the time after the birth of a child. Hasn't anyone ever heard of self-control?

Am I saying that pleasure in the sex act within marriage is sin? *No!* I am saying that the *emphasis* on pleasure has overshadowed the simplicity of God's intentions. If anything, this new emphasis on pleasure and the right to orgasm has artificially raised expectations for sex to the point that it has fueled the evangelical divorce rate.

A Little Leaven

Sandra was thrilled with anticipation. Her life had been a mad ride until she finally surrendered to Christ. She'd been through two marriages and had two children. The Singles Conference appeared to be just what she needed—she could learn the *Christian* way to be single.

Her auburn hair glittered in the spring morning light as she entered the huge suburban church. The nearly new edifice housed one of the fastest growing churches in the region. The open beam foyer was flooded by the brilliant sunrise colors that burst through the two-story plate glass windows. This church, in a short time, had become known for its ministries to almost every conceivable need.

Sandra was expecting good things when she selected the "Sexuality and Singleness" workshop. She clearly understood the proper role of sex from just reading her Bible, but she was sure that Larry, the workshop teacher, would be able to bring additional light to bear.

Larry was in his mid-thirties and good-looking in a baby-faced way. His glib manner was disarming and Sandra settled in comfortably, in spite of the metal folding chairs, to listen.

Sandra began to feel some discomfort as Larry began to explain, "We are sexual creatures. God made us that way." Had he left off there, his jocular manner would have carried it off, but he added, "God understands our sexual needs — the needs of our God-given sexual nature." Sandra was a little confused. It didn't sound like anything she'd read in the Bible in the last several months since her salvation.

Larry walked to the easel as he cast out another of his witty sayings. While the chuckle went through the audience, he uncovered the chart that listed the various stages of sexual contact from hand-holding to breast-fondling to intercourse. He began to show the progressive nature of these steps and how each corresponded to a different stage in the "relationship."

Sandra felt embarrassed as she saw that actual intercourse was the only one absolutely reserved for marriage. He had seemed so smooth a speaker; she had not been ready for a direct challenge to what she believed the Bible taught. Sandra was scratching her head when she left the room. Her spirit was troubled. "How could a church let someone like that teach?" she wondered. She looked around at the plush building that had so inspired her confidence before. The appearance was somehow altered.

"*A little leaven*," she said to herself as she left the church building.[21]

⁂   ⁂   ⁂

Today some of the deterioration is more visible, as in this 1989 singles' conference example. Instead of the church being salt and light to Western civilization, it seems that the church had elected to become pupil to the barbarians within.

> Have orgasms and bubble baths and wine created a sexual revolution among fundamentalists? Is a newly discovered zeal for mutually satisfactory sex capable of transforming a way of life based on literal interpretation of the Bible, strict adherence to authority, and the submission of women? In many ways, today's pro-sex Christian leaders seem to have absorbed the messages of the women's sexual revolution into their authoritarian culture.[22]

And this leaven has made Marabel Morgan's *Total Woman* acceptable. But, returning to the principle of escalation, *Total Woman* wasn't total enough.

It wasn't long before the human, carnal nature soon stripped the gears of the comparatively slow-moving and *simple* pleasures of sex promoted by the Wheats and the demure, sanctified bump-and-grind of the *Total Woman*.

Soon the evangelical market was flooded with Christian sex manuals which almost seemed to be contending for the sexier-than-thou award. Moral Majority board member, Rev. Tim LaHaye, who co-authored a manual[23] with his wife, Beverly, showed them all that "moral people could have fun, too." Where the Wheats found no Scripture against oral sex, the LaHayes were ambivalent but warned about possible problems. Clifford and Joyce Penner, in *The Gift of Sex,* gave their approval to oral sex, pulling handily ahead of the pack of sexy ministers. But their title as the Western world's sexiest Christians was quickly in question as their offering was eclipsed by *Celebration in the Bedroom*[24] by Rev. Charles and Martha Shedd which introduced anal sex into the Christian sexual arsenal.[25] These two progressives literally flabbergasted the LaHayes on a Donahue show by candidly admitting to owning "a whole drawerful" of vibrators.[26] Meanwhile, the societal pimps cackled with delight.

But there has been a backlash to the mounting heap of Christian sex books. Some old "fuddy-duddies" still hold the line. And there is even positive movement toward a revival of Biblical standards for marriage and sex. *The Way Home*[27] by Mary Pride has begun a virtual revolution which appears to be swelling up from those weary of the ceaseless chase of being culturally "with it" as Christians. Mary's follow-up, *All The Way Home,*[28] is threatening to blow the lid off of the satanic sales campaign — and add to the numbers of Christian babies as well.

Yet the church's sexual frontiers still appear wide open. The good intentions of the Marabel Morgans and the Dr. and Mrs. Wheats to help Christians relax a little about sex have been turned to swill by the leaven of the sex-for-pleasure heresy.

The Church in the Pink

"How blessed and favored you are that God has made you Gay! He has given you an honor that far exceeds that of childbearing. He has exalted you above the angels by giving you a place in heaven that is the highest among men. He has given you a heavenly song that only you can sing" (Father Thomas, "An Open Letter to a Gay Christian," Everett, Washington).[29]

I have deliberately used this extreme example to illustrate the direction that the church in the West is moving with regard to homosexuality. A few years ago it would have been ludicrous for *anyone* to attempt a connection between Christianity and sodomy. Yet today we see whole "churches," such as the Metropolitan Community Church (formerly, The First Church of Sodomy) given to homosexuals. Admittedly, these are a fringe element—for now. Many of the older, less Biblically sound churches have made a place for homosexuals and proclaim them "normal."

But even the more conservative churches are beginning to erode the edges of where sin begins. Many churches are beginning to accept that homosexuality is unchangeable, which is a direct denial of the power of the cross of Christ. Some feel that the orientation toward same-sex arousal happens too early or too mysteriously to discover and counteract, while others have bought the lie that homosexuality is an inborn condition. Despite the fact that there have been *no* studies that have indicated this, well-known Christian leaders such as Tony Campolo feel compelled to say, "More and more research suggests that in a great number of cases, if not the overwhelming majority, homosexual orientation is inborn."[30]

While Campolo insists that homosexual behavior is sin, he leaves these hapless people trapped with an irreconcilable drive to sin and no escape. Scripture does not treat any other sin or sinful lifestyle in this manner. Christ promised forgiveness and freedom.

Is it any wonder that homosexuals reject churchborne "solutions?" It would be like admitting that they were nitrogen-breathers and dooming themselves to breathing only oxygen or nothing at all. That there is no other sinful practice that has been treated this way by the Western church testifies to the success of the homosexual movement in confusing the basic issues with talk of "orientation."

Yet, we do not see someone with a "lying orientation" and spend years trying to ferret out the reasons for it. Nor do we look for a "lying gene" or "lying enzyme" to excuse the "victim." Neither do we leave them stranded in hopelessness. We insist on repentance, offer all the help we can, and expect their consistent progress in leaving sin behind.

Yet the Western church has begun to nibble on this "orientation" bait and threatens to swallow it whole. Even this, though, would not be the end of the downward seductive trail it travels. The church has been following the world on its tour of degeneracy, usually only a few years behind. If it continues, it will be the fatal dart in the liver of Western civilization. Will the church tour the final exhibit of "liberation" — the sexualization of children?

What We Have Seen

- The church entered this century with the delusion that love was an emotion which led to marriage.

- Later, when the church began to accept birth control, the purpose for sex was destroyed.

- There was little argument against premarital sex except pregnancy and disease — and those were eventually eliminated.

- Many Christians accepted the naturalistic belief that teens, especially boys, needed to release sexual tensions and used this belief to justify masturbation.

- An influx of former hippies, now Christians, who retained false notions of "love" as emotion and sex, entered the ministry.

- The church began to adopt a new purpose for sex — pleasure — but defined it with terms such as becoming *one flesh* and *intimacy.*

- Christian sex manuals began to appear and teach pleasure techniques.

- The natural, carnal process of escalation began to affect the sexual appetites of Christians, and the demand for new sexual experiences grew instead of reaching a level of satisfaction.

- The secular sex-liberationists gloat over the leavening effect they have had on the church.

- There are signs of a revival of scriptural concepts of marriage and sex.

What We Will See

Not only is revival possible — it has begun! It begins with a fresh look at what God wants from marriage and sex. We were made for *His* pleasure. What does the Bible say about these things? What is the place of pleasure, romance, and emotion?

Once we begin to understand the proper view of these things, how will that affect our behavior? How can we implement our newfound understanding into daily living?

What specific things can we do to begin to free our culture from the satanic skin trade? How can we shape the battle of the future, the ongoing war with Satan for the heart of Western civilization?

10

GOD, MARRIAGE, AND SEX: THROWING OFF THE SHACKLES

It must have been an ill-marked day in hell's kitchen where the lusty demons were cooking up another dose of sex perversion for the Western church. It must have been an ill-marked day when Mary Pride, sitting amid the teetering stacks of written and rewritten chapters and still eyeing her children, typed these words, "I'm almost afraid to ask this, because family planning has become as American as motherhood and apple pie *used* to be—but I have to. *If children are a blessing, why don't we want to have them?*"[1]

It *was* an ill-marked day. But hell's minions were too busy gleefully stirring up their vile concoctions to notice the Missouri housewife setting the torch to their carefully constructed Love Myth and calling God's saints to account. Her words seemed so tiny on that typewriter — such insignificant words — but when they were published, a tremor began.

≈   ≈   ≈

Mary Pride said nothing new. In fact, she said something old — something old and *lost*. Others had stood for old Christian standards but scarcely understood why. Others knew what Mary knew but knew not how to say it.

It had been a long time since anyone had clearly and cogently argued the ancient teaching of the church on marriage and sex from *Scripture*.

Quite simply, the lie was exposed for all its perversity and rottenness and, as one Christian leader told me, one would have to go "outside of Scripture" to argue against her conclusions.

The Love Battle

Briefly, I will clear one thing. Love is *not* an emotion. It is *not* indefinable. It is *not* something you fall in, the poets and songwriters notwithstanding. Love is something you *choose* to *do*.

Jesus did not command us to feel good about our neighbors or our enemies. He commanded something infinitely harder. He told us to *love* them, to *do* for them what was God's best for them, whether we felt like it or not.

In the Beginning It Was Not So

The people thronged about the ordinary, even somewhat homely man who sat on the low wall surrounding the village well. Low murmurs of apprehension rose from the group as the Pharisees approached with their brows properly knitted with looks of concern. The crowd parted like the Red Sea before the staff of Moses, and the Pharisees moved to stand before the teaching Galilean.

He squinted as He looked up into their faces; the glaring afternoon sun was at their backs. He had stopped teaching as soon as they arrived and seemed to be patiently waiting for their question — almost as though He knew it already.

"Is it lawful," one said with an edge of challenge in his voice, "for a man to divorce his wife for any cause at all?"

A low whisper passed through the gathering crowd as they exchanged meaningful glances. The Galilean allowed a slight grin to surface briefly on His face. He looked at the Pharisees and then at the people gathered in the dusty square. Then, as though reciting the simplest of Shabbat lessons, He said to the learned clan, "Have you not read, that He who created them from the beginning 'made them male and female,' and said, 'For this cause a man shall leave his father and mother, and shall cleave to his wife; and the two shall become one flesh?'

"Consequently they are no longer two, but one flesh. What therefore God has joined together, let no man separate."

The imperious Pharisees were stunned. The attentive listeners responded with a titter and a few guffaws. "But," replied one Pharisee, "why did Moses command us to give a writing of divorce and send her away?"

The teacher locked in on the inquisitor's eyes and pity filled His own as He said, "Because your hearts are hard — that's why Moses permitted it. But from the beginning it was not so . . ." (see Matthew 19:3–9).

In Jesus' time, the great debate was on divorce. One camp held that divorce was never permissible — understandably a small camp — while the other, larger group held that divorce was possible for any cause. The world around them was pagan and perverse, but, through hellenization, the Jews had allowed much corruption into their own lives. Their cunning and articulate questions were met by Jesus with the Word of God, but not with just *any* verses. Jesus went to the beginning, where *God's* intention was displayed.

In the legal world, He would be said to be relying on *precedent*. Only this was the ultimate in precedent: the demonstrated ideal of God for creation.

I believe that Jesus' method can be relied upon as valid and I intend to use such precedent as foundational proof. Realizing that a great many beliefs often stand or fall on a single premise, this will play a large role in discovering God's intention for marriage and sex, which will ultimately affect many other parts of our lives.

What Hath God Wrought?

To begin with, I will presuppose that God hates divorce, since He actually says that, and that He created marriage as a bond between two, one male, the other female, for life. As one radio teacher put it, "One man, one woman, and no *spares*." This was the teaching of Jesus. I also believe that there is an *extremely limited* justification in the cases of adultery or abandonment.[2]

One of the first things that God called "not good" was that man was alone. Modern teachers leap on this to show that man needs companionship or "intimacy" in relationship. This, the new guidebooks say, is the reason for marriage. I submit that Adam had all the companionship and relationship he could *ever* want or need in God Himself.

Only after Adam named the animals was this "aloneness" fully demonstrated. At this point, the big difference between man and the other creatures was that they had received the command and the capability to "be fruitful and multiply." This was not the case with Adam. So the Lord's comment that it was not good for man to be alone was deliberately punctuated by the naming of all these animals who already had mates, followed by the remark, "but for Adam there was not found a helper suitable for him."[3] It is almost as though God and Adam had been searching for a "helper," not a companion or intimate friend. It implies that the *animals* all had "helpers."

One might well ask what an animal had need of help *doing*. They only *had* one command: be fruitful and multiply.

Well, there wasn't a helper for Adam, so God made Eve and brought her to him who, immediately recognizing a good thing, said, "This is it!" God then goes on to say the words that Jesus quoted about the two being one flesh.

Here's where the waters divide, though. It seems that the Christian sex manuals would almost imply that God immediately added, "Why don't you kids just go and have a good time! And don't forget the condoms." In reality, God blesses them and says, "Be fruitful, and multiply [You mean right away? Before my career is underway?], and replenish the earth [That many, huh?]" (Genesis 1:28).

He doesn't seem to have a lot of instructions for Adam about Eve's "right" to be "loved to orgasm" or good stewardship over how many children "they can properly train to serve God."

God created the sex act, which does not need orgasm, pleasure, *or even marriage to occur.* The Apostle Paul warns against Christians becoming "one flesh" with harlots. He even indicates that since the believer is one with the Lord, that it horribly connects Christ with that sin (see 1 Corinthians 6:15–16).

The unity happens through the sex act itself. And God didn't create Adam and Eve and Gina and Betty and . . . nor did He create Adam and Steve and . . . nor did he leave Adam alone. This has got to tell us something about the nature of marriage and sex. Namely, as Jesus wisely pointed out, that God had something very specific in mind.

I also suspect that part of God's cure for Adam's aloneness can be found in what He knew would be the *natural result* of presenting Adam with a female counterpart: children. In fact, that is what He *commanded* them to do: be fruitful and multiply. And if there was ever a cure for feeling alone, it's children!

But this unity and these children were not created *primarily* for Adam and Eve, but for God Himself. As much as it hurts our dignity to remember it, God created everything for *His* pleasure.[4] God has many desires and plans, but in the end all things will be unto *His* glory. If we struggle with *that* concept, we need to reevaluate our understanding of God.

What I mean to say is that *God* had His own reasons for "making the two, one." He had His *own* plan for unity and childbearing that was quite apart from whether sex was fun, or staying married was fashionable, or having children was considered good stewardship. In Malachi 2, God is berating Judah for their attention to religious detail while they "deal treacherously" with their wives. He says, "Has not the LORD made them one? In flesh and spirit they are his. And why one? *Because he was seeking godly offspring*"[5] (emphasis added).

Now God doesn't always spell out His own purposes so clearly, but this tells us that it is *God* who wants the children. And if His instructions on rearing children gives us any hint, He wants them raised in such a way that they will bring *Him* glory. Many times God has staked out the procreation territory as exclusively His by deciding whose womb to open or close — and when. It seems the height of arrogance for *us* to decide when and how often we will bear *His* children.

Some people may think God was just kidding with all His talk of children numbering as the stars of the heavens and the sands of the seashore, but I don't think so. God's intention is to *communicate,* not hide, His will.

So, by definition and example, marriage is two of God's people, a man and a woman, becoming one for the purpose of producing children to be raised unto God's glory.

Some of the Mystery Is Revealed

"But the rule is so . . . so . . . *arbitrary,*" he said intently. "Why *should* I be forced to put a guardrail around this balcony?"

His friend shrugged. "Well, it *is* thirty stories up, you know."

The builder looked agitated. He rolled his eyes heavenward and said through his teeth, "What has *that* got to do with it?"

"Well," remarked the friend almost sheepishly, "that's the way it has been done for a long time. Some say it is dangerous to step beyond the edge."

"Oh-h-h, no-o-o," cried the builder. "Not that old stuff! What'dya think — somebody'll *fall?* Maybe you even believe in *gravity,* huh?"

ва   ва   ва

Sometimes people need to understand the basis for a rule before the rule makes sense. But violating a rule you do not understand can be as deadly as deliberate rebellion against one you do. The code requiring guardrails on high places is a clear acknowledgement of the power and danger inherent in the law of gravity. The codes themselves, however, do not even mention that gravity is a presumption, even though it is. Not mentioning it does not mean the code is not connected to the law of gravity. But for someone who did not acknowledge the law of gravity, it would be difficult to defend the code.

In very much the same way, the church through the last few centuries, and especially in recent decades, has tried to defend marriage and sexual purity without understanding the basic laws — God's purposes.

If God's purpose for marriage and sex is unity and children to His glory, then prohibitions against adultery *make sense* simply because it violates the unity God created. Laws against homosexuality, bestiality, and masturbation become understandable since they are utterly unfruitful and there is no unity. Homosexuality is *more* than unnatural. It strikes at the heart of God's design in marriage. With an understanding of God's purposes, we Christians do not merely oppose homosexuality arbitrarily on the basis of "who they love" (as they are fond of saying), but because their activities and lives are an assault on God's purpose.

God's desire for unity and to have the children raised to His glory has caused Him to confine sex to marriage. God's opposition to sex outside of marriage is directly related to the sex act itself. God has placed sexual activity where it can be properly used. Dr. James Dobson has described sex as similar to a river which, kept in its banks, yields great good, but overflowing them, destroys. The key thing that is destroyed is God's purposes. God has never opposed premarital, extramarital, or perverse sex on the basis of the danger of disease or pregnancy, but on the basis of His desires.

Intercourse itself defines "oneness of flesh," not the orgasm of two individuals. Completed sex acts that are not concluded as intercourse amount to mutual masturbation—not unity. They also, like the use of condoms or other birth control, delete the possibility of pregnancy—another departure from God's purpose. Deliberately thwarting either of these two purposes is not in keeping with a Christian view of marriage and sex.

Does this mean we should *avoid* orgasm or pleasure? Of course not! *God* created pleasure and it is good. But it should never supplant God's purpose.

However, the authors of some Christian sex manuals like to quote Hebrews 13:4 which says, "Marriage is honourable in all, and the bed undefiled" and proclaim that what goes on between husband and wife is automatically "undefiled." First, this interpretation does not align with the purpose of marriage and sex "in the beginning." Such a reading would justify sadomasochism, anal sex — *absolutely anything.* Literally applied, the activity would not have to be *mutually* pleasurable so long as it was done in the "undefiling" aura of the marriage bed. The above quote also omits the end of the verse, "but whoremongers and adulterers God will judge." I think we need to call for proper context. A much better reading can be found in a good interlinear New Testament:[6] "Honorable [let] marriage [be held] in every [way], and the bed [be] undefiled; but fornicators and adulterers God will judge."

This reading seems to be telling married people to hold or possess their own marriage in an honorable way and let the marriage bed be *kept* undefiled. Then the last part of the verse makes more sense. If you try to include fornication (general sexual sins) or adultery (sex with others than your spouse) in your marriage, God will judge you.

Birth control is another area where the church has gone off the deep end. It wasn't until the 1930s that the first Christian denomination finally took the step of condoning birth control.[7] Before that, they all agreed that it was wrong, but they were hard-pressed to explain just *why.* By then, they had all but forgotten why

Scripture said marriage and sex existed. But, looking again at God's purpose, it is easy to see that birth control itself was askew. After all, God never rescinded or mitigated the order to be fruitful and multiply.

A "right" to birth control — a "right" to control fertility — is necessary to the justification of abortion. If one has a right or duty to choose number and spacing of children, then abortion becomes a legitimate backup plan for failed birth control. With the sanctity of the marriage act subverted, the sanctity of life itself is undermined.

Of course, abortion violates this basic teaching as well as the principle that man is made in God's image and innocent blood should not be shed. Surrogate parenting, in-vitro fertilization, and a host of other "complex issues" are well answered by their violations of and tamperings with the unity and fruitfulness purposes.

A lot of "hard cases" about sex could be answered by asking, "Is it capable of resulting in pregnancy?" and, "Is this the result of unity in sexual intercourse between a man and his wife?"

Is This the Return of the Killjoy God?

Immediately some of you are imagining a bunch of "Christian women" in frumpy, ankle-length dresses, no makeup, pinched faces, and eyes that look narrowly upon their husbands when they ask their wives to "do their duty."

Human beings are creatures of extremes. Either they think they must have unlimited license or be totally bound. You either agree to stop *all* forest cutting or you are *for* destroying the environment; either you favor *unilateral* disarmament or you *want* World War III; either you favor *sanctions* against South Africa or you *applaud* apartheid. But these dichotomies seldom exist in real life and are often merely polemics of the ongoing debate.

Some will undoubtedly imagine that my saying that pleasure is not a *purpose* of sex is the same as saying one *should not enjoy* sex. They couldn't be more wrong. But then, what am I saying *is* the place of emotion, romance, and pleasure in marriage and sex?

Here's a good illustration. What is the *purpose* of eating? Most would agree that nourishment to support life would be the correct answer. I would add that God's purpose for eating continues from merely supporting life to glorifying Him with that life. While it is true that someone could fulfill that purpose with oatmeal and some vitamins, most would feel that it was a rather austere view of the purpose of eating. But if it came to being stranded on a deserted isle with a lifetime supply of Quaker Oats and One-a-Day vitamins, few would opt for starvation. The fact is that much of the world's population has little in the way of variety in their daily food, and they are not terribly concerned about that so long as they can eat at all.

Will anyone imagine in my saying that food is for nourishment unto a life pleasing to God, that I am opposed to *flavor?* Probably not, but I am willing to predict that there are those who will finish this book still believing that I oppose loving emotions and pleasure in sex.

Yet, if someone were to say that the purpose of food was *flavor,* you would probably balk at that, especially if they began touting an inalienable "right to be fed until the palate experiences a gourmet's delight" or that "flavor is a feeling and no Christian diner should endure eating without it."

Now, how would it sound to you if I offered you nightshade berries, which are highly poisonous, and I explained that I could just *feel* that they would be good. Further suppose that they actually had a pleasant taste. If you, knowing what they were, ate them based on my *feelings* and the taste alone, you would have a very strange way of choosing food. Would that be a perversion of the purpose of eating? Of course!

God, had He been a real killjoy, could have made everything taste like oatmeal. Instead He blessed us with an incomprehensible variety of things to mix and match, blend and stir, and roll together. The variety mentioned in the Bible alone is utterly astounding. But I think I would be safe in saying that eating nothing but flavored styrofoam, no matter how good-tasting, would be a perversion since there is no possibility of nourishment. We even recognize a similar distortion in bulimia, in which someone wants to eat but seeks to avoid the nourishment by inducing vomiting after eating.

Like any other good thing, Satan has innumerable ways to pervert it from its intended purpose. This has been the case with marriage and sex.

In *The Way Home,* Mary Pride discusses what she calls "sexual gluttony" in the chapter wonderfully titled, "The Joy of Unkinky Sex." "Gluttony," she asserts, "can be defined as *seeking an experience to such an extent that the basic purpose of one's actions is ignored or perverted*" (emphasis added).[8] Some Christian sex manuals illustrate this definition perfectly. Page after page in these tomes is devoted to how to escape the little complications, children, while you're enjoying this orgasmic Disneyland. Throughout all these anti-parenthood pamphlets, there is almost no word about the *abortive* nature of many of these methods. Deliberate sterility just for fun. What a perversion!

If we establish that God's purpose in marriage and sex is unity and procreation, we should have no trouble defining the limits of pleasure, emotion, and romance. They are all wonderful things, but they are not the thing itself. They are subsidiary to God's purposes. But let us test the ground here a little more.

Is emotional love necessary for marriage to take place? If it were, then the majority of all past marriages would have failed, and modern America would have the lowest divorce rate in world history. Early Christians were almost exclusively married by arrangement. Sometimes there may have been emotional links between the couple before the marriage, other times they had never met, but their divorce rate was nearly nil. They knew there was more to the marriage than the temporary passions of young people.

In theory, and most of the time in practice, arranged marriages or ones requiring parental permission were based on parents' being many years wiser than the child. As such, the parents were able to select a young man or woman for their child who was Christian, had shown good character, had a trade, and a number of good attributes. They were able to spot potential problems too. Boys and girls were raised with the expectation of building love, starting at the altar. Love was defined as a commitment to giving, not an expectation of receiving. This idea fits well with God's purpose in marriage.

But romantic literature is strewn with fathers giving their beautiful daughters to hoary, old misers only to have the dastardly plan foiled by the power of "true love." There probably were cases of arranged marriage where the parents' only concern was financial, but this, too, was a perversion of God's purpose.

The next question is: Is emotional love necessary to keep a marriage together? My answer is that if it were, no marriage would survive. Consider how much time a married couple spends *feeling* their love for one another. The husband is at the garage or the office concentrating on loving his wife and family by his commitment to earning a living for them. If he spent time mooning over his *feelings* about them, he would open that drain plug in the oilpan, and the stream of oil would likely end up in his mouth. Or he would rest his hand on the computer keyboard as he gazed out the window thinking of them and enter line upon line of "hhhhhhhhhhhhhhhhhhhhhhhh" onto the screen. The wife's work wouldn't turn out much better. This does not mean there are never feelings involved, but sometimes it is the emotion of anger, not love, that is present, and it takes *real* love to override that.

Even sex itself comprises such a small portion of married lives that we would be better off focusing our attentions elsewhere. But I am not recommending the chronic pulse-taking method of fussing over the "relationship." That kind of marriage has become so introspective as to be dangerous. As a cure for the introspective blues, I recommend an application of Mary Pride's *All The Way Home*[9] and regular doses of her quarterly magazine, *HELP*.[10]

I can't help but believe that marriages are far better off if we "prefer one another in love" rather than "falling" in love, especially when we define love unselfishly by 1 Corinthians 13 rather than defining it by how we feel. If utter dedication and whole-minded love is our goal in reading the Song of Solomon rather than the purely physical aspects of the passages, we have gained.

Unity is *not* measured by orgasm, nor is love by feelings. Unity is a fact of God's creation, whether the couple enjoys the experience or not. Otherwise inexperienced newlyweds may go for years without becoming "one."

> Let your fountain be blessed,
> *And rejoice in the wife of your youth.*
> As a loving hind and a graceful doe,
> Let her breasts satisfy you at all times;
> *Be exhilarated always with her love.*
> (Proverbs 5:18-19 NASB, emphasis added)

This thrilling and tender word comes to you from God, the one you thought was a killjoy. This is the emotional love I have written about in this book but with a difference.

The Christian concept of man was that there was a descending rank starting with God, to man's spirit, to man's soul, and then to his body. Emotions have to be subservient to God's purpose and to man's rational decisions. In other words, man can and should direct his emotions, not the other way around.

Now look again carefully at the lines of the Proverb above that tell the man to rejoice in his wife. It does not ask, nor plead, but *tells.* It also does not say that the wife will *make* him rejoice by wearing cellophane, Fredrick's of Hollywood black lace lingerie, or by dressing like a spy. This man is being told to *cultivate* his satisfaction and exhilaration by *choosing* to rejoice in her. Evidently, God expects us to control our emotions by choosing them.

Earlier in the chapter I said that love is not an emotion but a choice. Here is the chance to have the blessing of chosen love and a growing exhilaration. The same God who proclaimed that children are a blessing also said, "He who finds a wife finds a good thing, and obtains favor from the LORD."[11] If a wife is a good thing, we ought to rejoice.

The husband is responsible for kindling, rekindling, and maintaining the flame of his emotions and desires. God commands that he focus this exhilaration exclusively on his wife.

I can't think of anything that would make a wife happier than a husband who really rejoiced and praised God for her — one that was constantly cultivating that deep joy, satisfaction, and exhilaration in her.

What We Have Seen

- The church must reassess its foundational understanding of God's purpose in love, marriage, and sex.

- Jesus' method of Scripture proof by using "first things" as precedent is valid.

- By this means we can see that God intended:
  (a) Marriage to be one man, one woman, no spares.
  (b) That the two be one flesh.
  (c) That they be fruitful and multiply.
  (d) That both unity and procreation be through sexual intercourse.
  (e) That all these be for the purpose of furthering God's glory.

- Many of God's commands make more sense in light of correctly understanding basic truths.

- Prohibited sexual behaviors are those that do not fulfill one or both of God's purposes for marriage and sex — unity and procreation.

- The places of emotion, romance, and pleasure are subsidiary to unity and procreation.

- Love is not an emotion but a choice to do what is best for another.

What We Will See

We can change our own thinking. But can we change our nation or our culture? Do we even want to?

In the next chapter, we will reveal the "sinister" plot by God to take over America — and not just America, but Western civilization and *the world*. We will explore what you can do practically, if you are still a slave to the skin trade or if you know someone who is. We will see what movements are happening now to turn the tide and show you how to become involved.

Finally, there will be a list of recommended books and organizations that will start you on your way to being a true Christian soldier, bent on liberating others from the skin trade.

11

A CHRISTIAN AMERICA,
A CHRISTIAN WEST,
A CHRISTIAN WORLD:
SPREADING
THE FREEDOM

The dark-haired electrician leaned back in the chair at his desk. His fingers were casually laced behind his head. We were just winding up one of our regular, rapid-fire discussions of issues from abortion to pornography, prostitution to homosexuality.

He was interesting to argue with because he really *thought* about issues instead of throwing out bumper-sticker positions.

He grinned easily and said, "Well, Christian or not, you've got as much right to influence the laws as anyone else."

I chuckled inwardly, watching his mouth go slack as I said, "Influence? Christians don't want to influence. We want to take over!"

₰   ₰   ₰

Jesus said, "Go therefore and make disciples of all the nations, baptizing them in the name of the Father and the Son and the Holy Spirit, teaching them to observe all that I command you; and lo, I am with you always, even to the end of the age."[1]

In this, Jesus was not asking us to try to influence a few people around us. He was pointing us toward the world and saying, "Go get 'em, boys!" Naturally, He wasn't fomenting violent revolution; we were to exert the pressure of godly influence and be as leaven. But the goal was that Christ Himself would be exalted as King of kings in nations and cultures as well as individual lives. We all look to the day when Jesus will be acknowledged as King, when He shall return in person. In the meantime, however, we are to spread His kingdom until nations know and obey His ways. We are to *occupy* until He comes, occupy in the military sense — take the ground and keep it!

Through the intervening centuries, the leavening has worked well. But there has been opposition, there have been setbacks. The entire world picture has changed. The West has become the acknowledged world leader, and it has primarily been as a result of the Christianization of Western civilization. True science began in the West because Christianity taught that

God was rational and orderly and that the universe could be studied and known. Hospitals and nursing orders originated in the West because Christianity taught that every man's life was valuable. Slavery was attacked and eliminated in the West because Christianity taught that all men were equal before God. Human sacrifice was done away with because Christianity taught that God wished to save *all* men and that Jesus was a sufficient offering for men's souls. Republics with constitutions began in the West because Christianity taught that even the king or emperor was under law.

Today, in the West, no religion is taken seriously unless it proclaims love, mercy, and kindness. Eastern religions are forced to adopt these virtues in order to be considered as religions by Western man. Even many of the atheists, agnostics, and humanists do not realize that they are totally under Christian influence when they debate against us and talk of "equality," "fairness," "compassion," and "freedom." The brutal, demagogic regimes of ancient, pre-Christian times are the exception, not the rule, in the West. No claims of perfection here, but a lot has been accomplished by dogged insistence on truth from God's Word.

But, as I've asserted, we have been romanced into some dangerous compromises through the centuries, and it is only beginning to tell on us in the last few decades. And somewhere we also lost the vision of a Christian America. We've been cowed into being ashamed of such thoughts. But God's purpose is a

Christian *world,* a project that starts with a fervent Christian person expanding to a dynamic Christian family turned loose in a powerful Christian church and exploding onto a Christian nation.

Our opposition, who shame us with the catcalls of *pluralism,* want not just a non-Christian America, but an anti-Christian America — a *religion-free* America. Why should we stand for such a brazen conspiracy? If the utterly despotic Roman Empire was no match for eleven uneducated Galileans who carried only the command of Christ to disciple the nations, why should we fear the chattering gaggles of humanists, atheists, and Marxists?

It is time to allow Jesus Christ to shatter our shackles of sexual slavery and carry the battle to the enemy's territory. Jesus said that the gates of hell would not prevail against His church (see Matthew 16:18). And when the church has gone on the offensive, those gates have been shaken and shattered every time.

> Awake, awake, clothe yourself in strength, O Zion; clothe yourself in your beautiful garments, O Jerusalem, the holy city. For the uncircumcised and the unclean will no more come into you. Shake yourself from the dust; rise up, O captive Jerusalem; loose yourself from the chains around your neck, O captive daughter of Zion. For thus says the LORD, "You were sold for nothing and you will be redeemed without money." (Isaiah 52:1-3 NAS)

Repentance: The Foundation of Restoration

Many have had to repent of activities in the slave market, whether it was entertaining impure thoughts or romping with prostitutes and homosexuals. But most now need to repent of inactivity. Even most of those in the church who were never involved in the skin trade were also never involved in stopping the slime. When we consider the command of Christ to teach the nations to observe all His commands, we are guilty of gross negligence and dereliction of duty at the very least.

It is not the legislators who are called to be salt and light (see Matthew 5:13–16); it is not the police, district attorneys, the Supreme Court, or the motion picture rating association. *We* are! We're the ones who are called, and we are not fulfilling that calling. We must repent of this apathy — repent of our culpability for all the lives devastated while we hold our peace. Their blood is on our heads.[2]

When I first became active as a Christian, the issue was abortion. I picketed, wrote, spoke, and informed people. But I was angry — angry at the abortionists, angry at the clinic escorts, and angry at the legal system. Of course, I was civil enough. I didn't yell, scream, or snort, but I blamed *them* for our deplorable state.

Not until God turned up the lights did I see that they were not to blame. They weren't saved; they were blind. I *was* saved. I had sight. I *knew* what abortion really was, and I had spent twelve years doing *nothing*.

The only reason abortion *could* have been legalized was because of Christian apathy. Christians and Christian ideas controlled Western civilization for centuries, and we gave up the reins without firing a shot.

What a self-righteous prig I was!

Only when I began to act out of repentance did I begin to have any real effect, because my attitude better reflected Christ. I believe that this principle will apply to *all* Christian activism from preaching the gospel, to picketing against porn, to legislative efforts to stop "gay rights," to blocking abortion clinic entrances. Just as Israel often needed national repentance, so, in order to war properly, the church in the West must begin to march on its knees.

A Free Man

Everyone had abandoned Sam to the grim fate of slavery—everyone except his wife and Jesus Christ. Even Sam nearly gave up on Sam.

"Why hasn't my being a Christian helped?" he wondered. His question drove him to seminary. Not to try to enter a ministry—he knew he couldn't do *that*—but to make a last desperate search for escape from the skin trade.

Here Sam rediscovered the Word of God. Here he discovered that simple resistance was useless. Now, when the Word said, "The heart . . . is desperately wicked" (Jeremiah 17:9), Sam *believed* it—he *knew* it.

He learned that Christ could set him free when his faith fell flat. But it was here that he also learned that he must submit himself to God and His Word. Resistance to sin was only possible from that position. He must choose to believe God without regard to his own thoughts and submit his life to the Word.

The chains began to break, the lash of the slaver began to fade. Daily, he and God met — he in abject submission. The gift of God, a loving wife, stood with Sam.

Sam is a free man.

Yes, this is the same Sam you met in chapter 9 — the one whose pastor had simply waved off Sam's addiction saying, "You'll grow out of it." But what Sam eventually discovered were four key elements[3] in overcoming, and none had anything to do with "growing out of it."

Steve Gallagher, founder of Pure Life Ministries, says, "Is there hope for the sexual addict? Can he *really* change? The answer is a resounding 'yes!' It has happened in my life and in the lives of countless others who have put their trust in God."[4]

But, as always, the trail starts with acknowledging our transgressions to God (see 1 John 1:9; Psalm 32:5). In our interview, Sam told me, "I had to fully realize how utterly depraved human nature is — how utterly depraved I was." First John 1:9 tells us that when we confess our sin, God will cleanse us from sin.

But as one preacher has said, "The blood of Jesus does not wash away excuses — only sins." Often we strive to mitigate the awfulness of sin or justify it with reasons why we fell — "I was really tired that day. I hadn't gotten enough sleep." But if you try to justify yourself, you leave no place for Jesus Christ to justify you.

But perhaps a more serious error is when we don't agree with God. *We* don't understand why God would prohibit *that*, so we plunge right in. If we do not accept that God is *always* right even if that makes *us* always wrong, then we will ultimately fail. God's Word must be accepted at face value as the *absolute* arbiter of right and wrong. Understanding the command, "flee fornication," is simple. Understanding *why* may take more time or never happen at all. But with or without understanding why, obedience is a must. This is what it means to submit to God.

After I came to Christ, I continued to live under many of my inculcated delusions. Quite simply, I was not aware of how much the twentieth-century paganism had molded me. But, by God's grace, I was confronted regularly in God's Word by the difference between what I assumed to be so and what God claimed was the truth. I had cold decisions to make. Would I begin to live according to God's stated truth? Would I do that in spite of the fact that I still mentally disagreed with that stated truth?

I decided that I must agree with the Apostle Paul and "let God be found true, though every man be found a liar"[5] — even if I was that liar. I decided to take no chances with sin; the stuff was simply too volatile. I could see why Jesus quickly followed up His denunciation of "just looking" at adultery with a call to radicalism. He said, "And if your right eye makes you stumble, tear it out, and throw it from you; *for it is better for you that one of the parts of your body perish, than for your whole body to be thrown into hell.*"[6]

In other words, it is better to go overboard on the side of fleeing sin than to risk sin's ultimate end. Of great value in fleeing sin is to cultivate the fear of the Lord, which Scripture says is "the beginning of wisdom" (Proverbs 9:10). This is not contradictory to the verse which says, "perfect love casteth out fear" (1 John 4:18). These two verses obviously use the word *fear* in a different way. It is especially critical to the sexual slave to have every tool available to flee sin. I recall many times in my early walk when my love for God was simply not enough to capture my mind from the hypnotic bait before my eyes. But a cold dash of eternal anger from God suddenly roused my sleeping strength to resist.

The simplest way to cultivate a pure fear of God is pray for it! I prayed many hours, asking God to allow me to have a glimpse of His awesome majesty. By reading of the men in Scripture who had such experiences, I knew holy fear accompanied such a glimpse. I asked for the fear of the Lord, and I thank Him for all that He gave me.

During those early years with Christ, these confrontations with the Word took place regularly, almost daily. And I still have to face myself in the mirror of God's Word today. There have been unpleasant consequences from my unwitting agreement with the world's

ideas. Some of my early poor decisions reflect the deception, but God has been gracious and mitigated some
of the worst results. Perhaps this was due to my willingness to submit to God's Word quickly. The lesson
of submitting to God, even when I didn't understand
the reasons, was one of the first things I learned as a
believer.

James gives us the proper sequence, "Submit your-
selves therefore to God. Resist the devil, and he will
flee from you."[7] I often hear this verse quoted only in
part as, "Resist the devil and he will flee from you."
Such a rendering is not only indefensible, it frustrates
those whose evil habits are the most ingrained. This
resisting is dependent on the willpower of men and not
the real power of God.

If you do not submit to God's Word, you will lose
the battle with the devil; he will simply outlast your
willpower.

Another applicable verse that is, again, tragically
half-quoted is, "You will know the truth, and the truth
shall make you free" (John 8:32 NAS). The implication
is that once you realize your enslavement and the possibility of freedom, you will become free. Nothing
could be further from the truth. The entire statement
from Jesus says, *"If you abide in My word,* then you
are truly disciples of Mine; and you shall know the
truth, and the truth shall make you free."[8]

This principle is very like the submit-resist combination of James with one important addition: The statement in John seems to say that there is a connection

between being obedient to the truth you already know and receiving more truth. In other words, if we are to escape the "culture blindness" we have about sexual slavery, we must begin by totally submitting to the truth we already know. Failure to be obedient to the truth God has already revealed will likely block any further revelation.

I know from personal experience that the sexual slave must, above all, submit *every* thought to God and be quick to call sin *sin*. This, of course, requires that you be continually refreshed by the Word of God so as to know what *God* calls sin. I was deeply impressed with this in my early Christian walk. When evil thoughts came, I spent *no time* at all trying to discern whether they were from the devil or my own mind. It was simpler and safer to take responsibility for their even being there and repent of them. I knew God would forgive my sins, but I was not sure that He would be so gracious about my trying to split hairs over the responsibility for my thought life. This was an example of how it was much safer to go overboard than to err in favor of sin. For the escaping slave, the slightest equivocation will be compounded beyond belief.

Escapees from the skin trade also need to distance themselves from what used to be called "occasions of sin." This means clearing out *all* the kinds of material and associations that lead your mind in those directions. This could be certain friends, pornography, romance novels, soap operas, off-color movies and videos, and even catalogues — *anything* that will stimulate those carnal thoughts. Ultimately the entire battle will depend on the willingness to courageously face the old, wicked taskmaster daily in his strongest territory: the mind.

The Ex-Slave's Revenge

As the believer begins to walk in freedom, his Lord will want him to take his place in the army of the Lord to carve out new territory from the enemy of our souls. A Christian's first "occupied territory" is his home.

> Now, therefore, fear the LORD and serve Him in sincerity and truth. . . . And if it is disagreeable in your sight to serve the LORD, choose for yourselves today whom you will serve . . . but as for me and my house, we will serve the LORD. (Joshua 24:14–15 NAS)

God created a family; governments and churches are all addendums. Later, when God gave His laws to Israel, He commanded *the parents* — not the judges or Levites — to teach the children godliness (see Deuteronomy 6:7).

Now it may be necessary for the ex-slave (now a pilgrim) to take lost ground that has been in enemy control. This may not be possible all at once, but every attempt must be made to set a standard of righteous behavior. Many homes will be utter wrecks after years of slavery, and some members may be content with their chains. Again, prayer and perseverance are required.

But realize that if it is the greatest revenge against Satan to be snatched out of his hands, then for you to make your family off-limits to him just punctuates the victory.

In cases where the family is willing to submit to God, the prospects are greater. Parents need to demonstrably begin to lead in submission to God's Word. Since the main carriers of the seduction are the media, those sources need to be severely limited and monitored or eliminated. We must teach our children to avoid the majority of the swill and to critically evaluate, according to the Word, what they cannot avoid.

In cases where the children are partly grown before the change in your life, it may only be possible to change the *direction* of the child's thinking. Even this, however, will make a significant difference to the next generation.

A free and pure family is the essential unit in the battle to turn Western civilization back to God. This is true because God designed sexuality to be properly contained in marriage.

Reclaiming the West

"Be sure to observe what I am commanding you this day: behold, I am going to drive out the Amorite before you, and the Canaanite, the Hittite, the Perizzite, the Hivite and the Jebusite. Watch yourself that you make no covenant with the inhabitants

of the land into which you are going, lest it become
a snare in your midst," the LORD told Israel.[9]

With this solemn warning, the Lord led Israel into
the Promised Land. The command was clearly to take
no prisoners! The reason was also clear: Israel would
be infected with their sin.

But Israel soon became weary of routing these enemies and discovered how useful the Canaanites could be
when put to forced labor.[10] Suddenly there were all
kinds of reasons *not* to drive out the enemy tribes. Soon
they were trading with them, then finally intermarrying
with them. In the end, they were enslaved by them.

Sound familiar? It should! When Western Christians stopped driving out all the enemies (sin), the excuses came easier. Then we had trade with and finally
sanctified some of the sin. Now we are slaves to this
sexualized culture.

But the battle is joined again. We may yet, by
God's grace, redeem what we have lost — only we can
give no quarter. Pluralism is *not* a virtue of God — *purity* is. The corruption has invaded all fronts: individual, home, church, nation, and world. All must be
fought relentlessly. "The earth is the LORD's and the
fulness thereof" (Psalm 24:1), and we have the opportunity to make that more apparent. "The fulness
thereof" includes political and social action — action
that reflects the purposes of God. It includes the arts,
journalism, government, and education. No area should
be untouched by God's people.

We should not be using the second coming of Christ to mask disobedience to His dictum that we be salt and light—that we make the gates of hell quiver and quake. To cloak apathy with Christ's return is blasphemy. Giving any ground to Satan is traitorous desertion. It makes a mockery of all Jesus commanded, and it leaves Satan's slaves stranded in the territories we refuse to attack.

Have I been such a deserter? You bet I have![11] I have deeply repented of the error, and God has been gracious to permit me into His service again.

The Word of God must be your weapon as you fight for today's ground. But the fight is not merely for today. Someone will inherit the future we leave them. Will we leave them a spiritual wasteland, the burnt-out hulk of a once-great civilization? Will we leave a second Dark Ages brought on by the wild rampages of the barbarians within? Or will we leave a larger, stronger army, still willing to wade into battle with the name of the Lord on their lips? Will we leave a vision of a Christ-centered civilization?

The Battle of the Future

"Like arrows in the hand of a warrior, so are children of one's youth. How blessed is the man whose quiver is full of them."[12] *Arrows?* I thought. I had always looked at the the part about being blessed by the full quiver—but *arrows?*

Suddenly it dawned on me. God has committed me to the battlefield of today using the sword, the Word of God, to take and defend the ground on which I stand. But when a soldier of that time was trying to move forward, the archers fired a hale of arrows into the next piece of ground. Just so, I could fight the *battle of the future* with my children. The better prepared they were, the more successful the future battle would be.

Not only will the future reflect the willingness of Christians to wage spiritual war today, but the future will depend on how well-made the arrows are that we launch into the future. If we neglect this vital arena, all our work will likely end with the death of this generation. Now is the time to instill the truths of Christ and the virtues of God in our children so that, not only will our gains be maintained, but they will be multiplied.

Franky Schaeffer rightly said, "The greatest act of positive Christian revolution today is the faithful husband and wife raising an informed and Christian family. The woman putting her children ahead of 'career' is today's last radical and real revolutionary for truth."[13] Probably one of the most effective ways of raising children unto the Lord is through homeschooling, which also acts as proof against the hoards of barbarians — administrators, teachers, and students, in the public schools.

You may feel inadequate to the task, but God has given *you* (not the school, the church, the day-care center, or the government) the job, and He will supply you grace to do it. It is a conspiracy of our time, consciously or unconsciously, to make parents feel like rank amateurs in rearing their children. It is particularly distressing when world-renowned Christian ministries that specialize in matters of family reflect this degraded view. In one case, an "expert" was asked if parents are qualified to teach their own children about sex, the response was, "Probably not." In her book on teaching your own children about sex, Connie Marshner says, "Contemporary American society has forgotten the wisdom of relying on parents as the major influence."[14] We should strive to remember it for our own children's sake.

It could take a long time to retrieve what Western civilization has lost, but it is our responsibility to retrieve it. The power is God's, but the sweat is ours.

You Are Not Alone

Elijah sat heavily on the rock under the parched juniper and gasped out a lungful of air. King Ahab's men were no doubt in hot pursuit and Elijah was exhausted. The shimmering heat of the ground before him made further flight look impossible. "Just let me die, Lord. I've done enough." Then he fell asleep.

Suddenly Elijah was wakened. Was it one of Ahab's men? No, it was an angel bidding him to eat. After a second meal from the angel, Elijah went another forty days—ending at Mt. Horeb, where he moved into a cave.

Solitary for days, Elijah soon began to despair. When the Lord asked him what he was doing, Elijah said, "I have been very zealous for the LORD God of hosts; for the sons of Israel have forsaken Thy covenant, torn down Thine altars and killed Thy prophets with the sword. *I alone am left,* and they seek my life."

God said, ignoring the self-pity, "I have 7,000 others who have not bowed to Baal" and sent Elijah on another mission.[15]

You may be tempted to feel alone in the fight, even in the midst of the church at times. But there are people and organizations who have already joined battle. There are books you should read to encourage and instruct you.

Some will see these resources as somewhat sparse, but the same was true of pro-life work just a few years ago. I believe that these represent the beginnings of a ground swell. I believe we can take heart from the pro-life movement. As it has grown, so, too, can a revival in sexual purity.

Below I have listed different areas we have discussed in the conflict. Under each are recommended reading and people to contact. It will be your responsibility to make use of these resources. These are *not* intended to be all inclusive, but as you become involved, you will find other contacts.

Sexual Addiction

For those enslaved by sexual sin or struggling with it I advise you to contact:

Steve Gallagher
Pure Life Ministries
P. O. Box 345
Crittenden, KY 41030
(606) 428-2255

Pure Life Ministries was started by Steve Gallagher, an ex-slave to the skin trade. He publishes a very cogent and helpful book called *Sexual Idolatry*. Get this book now! It could not come with a higher recommendation to the sexual addict. He can also show you how to start a local Pure Life group to meet the ever-growing group of runaway slaves. Pure Life's work is Christ-centered and aimed at helping porn addicts, homosexuals, users of prostitutes, and any other sexual bondage. Steve plays hardball when it comes to sappy psychological excuses for sin.

For those enslaved to homosexual lives, contact:

Exodus International/North America
P. O. Box 2121
San Rafael, CA 94912
(415) 454-1017

This is a truly international group that can put escaping homosexuals in touch with ex-homosexual Christian groups in Europe, North America, Australia, and other places. They are committed to changing homosexual tendencies, not merely gritting one's teeth and struggling through life. Their free, introductory packet lists North American referral and affiliate groups that must meet a list of requirements in order to be included.

There are other groups which maintain that homosexual orientation is unchangeable. I do not list them because this belief denies the power of Christ and leaves the homosexual hopeless.

I also recommend two other books which will provide some help for the bondservant of sin:

- *How to Say NO to a Stubborn Habit — even when you feel like saying Yes* by Erwin W. Lutzer (Victor Books, 1982). This is a simple, direct, and scriptural treatment of the subject of habitual sin.

- *Sensuality* by Charles R. Swindoll (Multnomah Press, 1981). This is a small, twenty-three page booklet that is very encouraging and shows how to handle temptation from the example of Joseph and Potiphar's wife.

Family Life

I'm sure you can guess what I will recommend here. There are three books you must read.

- *The Way Home* by Mary Pride (Crossway, 1985). This revolutionary volume gives more good reasons to rebel against the encroaching humanistic forces. It reveals and documents the subtle destructive power of feminist religion in the church.

- *All The Way Home* by Mary Pride (Crossway, 1989). This is a very practical book showing how to implement the discoveries in *The Way Home.*

- *The Bible and Birth Control* by Charles D. Provan (available from Zimmer Printing, 410 West Main St., Monongahela, Pennsylvania 15063). This fine little booklet defends from Scripture and church teaching the universal and timeless church (both Catholic and Protestant) position *against* birth control.

I also recommend signing up to receive the quarterly, *HELP* — an ultimately practical newsletter that helps mothers and fathers share insights on their childrearing task. For a year's subscription, send $15 to:

Home Life
P. O. Box 1250
Fenton, MO 63026-1250

Sane Sex

There are row upon row of sex manuals even in the Christian bookstores. Many stay on the best-seller list year after year. It is pretty hard to find someone who just wants to teach what God's Word says and show you how to pass on proper attitudes to your children. If you've been raised in the sexually inundated culture of today, it probably will teach you as well. This book comes highly recommended.

Decent Exposure: How to Teach Your Child About Sex by Connie Marshner (Wolgemuth & Hyatt, 1988).

Knowing Your Enemy: I Would Not Have You Ignorant

It is wise to know who is responsible for the bilge that is being pumped into our culture. There are several books that will open your eyes to the cultural pimps.

- *Grand Illusions: The Legacy of Planned Parenthood* by George Grant (Wolgemuth and Hyatt, 1988). This highly readable exposé of America's chief proponent of perversion is packed with usable facts and documentation.

- *The Home Invaders* by Donald Wildmon (Victor Books, 1985). This paperback shows how TV and other media are knowingly polluting our and our children's minds.

- *The Homosexual Network* by Enrique Rueda (Devin Adair, 1983). Documents the promotion of homosexuality in the West.

- *The Mind Polluters* by Jerry Kirk (Nelson, 1985). Pastor Kirk clears the boards on pornography and gives solid, usable information on how *you* can fight it in your own town and state.

- *Are Gay Rights Right?* by Roger J. Magnuson (Straitgate Press, Minneapolis, Minnesota, 1985). An update on the homosexual movement. Well-documented. Includes good resource list and tips on how to fight the "homosexualization" of America.

Home School

There are dozens of good books on homeschooling and many curriculums. Most Christian bookstores carry these. Steer clear of all the books on the mysterious malady of "home school burnout," which is most likely a case of being weary of well-doing (see Galatians 6:9; 2 Thessalonians 3:13).

If you need resources get:

The Big Book of Home Learning, The Next Big Book of Home Learning, and *Schoolproof* all by Mary Pride (Crossway). Yes, I *know* her name appears a lot, but she is a very busy lady who produces a lot of good work.

Preparation for Battle

Any soldier who wishes to succeed in battle will keep current on what is happening around him. But he must first be informed about the overall situation as well.

Here I will recommend some videotapes and publications to inform you on a number of issues. After this, I will list organizations that operate in these fields.

Videos

- *A Winnable War* from Focus on the Family (address below). This powerful video will give you a start in understanding how bad the pornography problem is in America.

- *Ted Bundy's Last Interview*, also from Focus on the Family. Serial killer Ted Bundy explains the role of pornography in shaping his criminal career.

Periodicals

- *American Family Association (AFA) Journal.* The AFA (address below) distributes this invaluable monthly resource. It is divided into sections for all the major moral issues. Especially covers obscene, indecent, and anti-Christian TV programming. Includes effective citizen action that can be taken such as writing to sponsors and boycotting products. Best all-around deal.

- *Citizen Magazine* from Focus on the Family. Well-written, informative monthly newsletter. Includes action suggestions.

- *The Teaching Home* is a bi-monthly Christian homeschoolers' magazine that will help you in the battle of the future. Excellent articles and reviews of teaching materials and methods. Legal news and a questions-and-answers column are also featured. About half the states in the U.S. have a local newsletter inserted into the magazine covering local home school situations. Very helpful!

Literature of the Resistance

- *A Christian Manifesto* by Francis Schaeffer (Crossway 1982). This is a bold challenge from a great modern theologian for Christians to act as salt and light in their culture.

- *The Great Evangelical Disaster* by Francis Schaeffer (Crossway 1984). Francis Schaeffer's parting shot documenting the modern capitulation to the world by the church.

- *A Time for Anger* by Franky Schaeffer, son of Francis Schaeffer, (Crossway 1982). A debunking of the "myth of neutrality" in the media and an agenda for Christian action to recapture the reins of Western society.

Organizations.

American Family Association
P. O. Drawer 2440
Tupelo, Mississippi 38803
(601) 884-5036

The AFA (formerly the National Federation for Decency) has been waging war against filth and moral decay for a long time. The media had branded the director, Rev. Donald Wildmon, as a nut for years — and an ineffectual nut at that. But recently the tide has shifted, and thanks to Wildmon's persistence and doggedly reliable reporting, people have begun to get involved. Major advertisers are backing out in droves from buying slots on slimy TV programs. Local chapter leaders are needed. They will also put you in touch with other local activists. The *AFA Journal* is a must.

Pure Life Ministries
P. O. Box 345
Crittenden, KY 41030
(606) 428-2255

This ministry to sexual addicts of all kinds has been growing slowly over the years and has much to offer. Starting a local chapter may be a good idea.

Morality In Media (MIM)
475 Riverside Dr.
New York, NY 10115
(212) 870-3222

MIM specializes in fighting obscenity and indecency in all media — TV, movie, and print. They have a legal department that will help when you are writing a model ordinance for your city or county or writing a new state law. They also have booklets outlining how to fight pornography in your area.

National Coalition Against Pornography (N-CAP)
800 Compton Rd., Suite 9224
Cincinnati, OH 45231
(513) 521-6227

N-CAP is nationally known as the spearhead of the clean-up of Cincinnati, Ohio. Through their vigilant efforts, obscenity laws are so strictly enforced there that there are *no* porno theaters or shops in Cincinnati. Only seven of the mildest porno magazines are even available in that city. Jerry Kirk, in his book, *The Mind Polluters,* tells you how to do it. They can assist you in finding other local activists.

Children's Legal Foundation
2845 E. Camelback Rd., Suite 740

Phoenix, AZ 85016
(602) 381-1322

Formerly Citizens for Decency through Law (CDL), this group will inform you on how to fight smut through legislative means. They have an excellent legal department that will check your legislative proposals for constitutionality and loopholes. Local chapters are available.

Focus on the Family
Pomona, CA 91799
(714) 620-8500

Dr. James Dobson has done us a great favor by sitting on the President's Commission on Pornography and then making us aware of the degradation of porn. Dobson's interests in social issues also includes abortion, homosexuality, and child abuse. His daily radio broadcasts (check local listings or contact Focus) often address these issues and recommend citizen action. *The Citizen* magazine from Focus deals strictly with these issues and suggested citizen action.

Steve Carr
Christian Connection
717 East Golf Road
Schaumburg, IL 60173
(312) 843-8855

Jim Fitzgerald
CTV Channel 40
Signal Hill Drive

Wall, PA 51548-1499
(412) 824-3930

Jeff Hanseler
Citizens for a Safe Pittsburgh
1990 Crafton Blvd.
Pittsburgh, PA 15205

These three people's names were supplied by
Focus on the Family's *Citizen* magazine as people who
can tell you how to develop a skillful and successful
local coalition to fight the "gay rights" forces.

Viva La Revolucion!

The old Marxists used to cry, "Proletariat, arise! You
have nothing to lose but your chains!"

This is the case for Western civilization, now
blinded and fettered in the skin trade. Since the good
that came from the West was of Christian inspiration,
it is the church's task to lead the return to sexual san-
ity. The revolution's single greatest weapons — the
Bible and prayer — are in our hands.

Whether the above resource books or groups agree
with all of my premises or not, they are the beginnings
of this revolution to overthrow the satanic taskmaster.
They are helping lead the exodus from the tyrant's
cruel grasp and will help give shape to the rebellion
against the cultural pimps.

As a body, the church must rise up to combat the
enslaver of this culture. As the church was used of

God in the past to bring blessing and freedom to the West, so should the church be used to restore it.

> Awake, awake,
>> put on strength, O arm of the LORD;
> Awake as in the days of old,
>> the generations of long ago.[16]

ENDNOTES

Introduction

1. C. S. Lewis, *Screwtape Letters*, (New York: Macmillan Publishing, 1980).

Chapter 1: Sold to the Skin Trade

1. The facts of the fourteen-year-old boy held in prostitution slavery in a Times Square hotel for six weeks, his escape and chase by the bottle-wielding pimp, and his dash to the safety of The Covenant House are true (*AFA Journal,* September 1987, 3). I have used my knowledge of Times Square in New York City and the Port Authority depot and my imagination to set the scene.

2. From the exclusive interview by Dr. James Dobson with serial sex killer Ted Bundy the day before his execution on January 24, 1989, for the murder of twelve-year-old Kimberly Leach. Bundy was implicated in the brutal slayings of dozens of young women in the U.S. (Focus on the Family tape, 1989).

3. Essay in *Gay Community News*. Also in the *Congressional Record,* February 15-21, 1987. The full text of this display of homosexual "tolerance" follows. This essay is bizarre, madness, a tragic, cruel fantasy, an eruption of inner rage, on how the oppressed desperately dream of being the oppressor.

We shall sodomize your sons, emblems of your feeble masculinity, of your shallow dreams and vulgar lies. We shall seduce them in your schools, in your dormitories, in your gymnasiums, in your locker rooms, in your sports arenas, in your seminaries, in your youth groups, in your movie theater bathrooms, in your army bunkhouses, in your truck stops, in your all-male clubs, in your houses of Congress, wherever men are with men together. Your sons shall become our minions and do our bidding. They will be recast in our image. They will come to crave and adore us.

Women, you cry for freedom. You say you are no longer satisfied with men; they make you unhappy. We, connoisseurs of the masculine face, the masculine physique, shall take your men from you then. We will amuse them; we will instruct them; we will embrace them when they weep. Women, you say you wish to live with each other instead of with men. Then go and be with each other. We shall give your men pleasures they have never known because we are foremost men too and only a man knows how to truly please another man.

All laws banning homosexual activity will be revoked. Instead, legislation shall be passed which engenders love between men.

All homosexuals must stand together as brothers; we must be united artistically, philosophically, socially, politically, and financially. We will triumph only when we present a common face to the vicious heterosexual enemy.

If you dare cry faggot, fairy, queer, at us, we will stab you in your cowardly hearts and defile your dead, puny bodies.

We shall write poems of the love between men; we shall stage plays in which man openly caresses man; we shall make films about love between heroic men which will replace the cheap, superficial, sentimental, insipid, juvenile, heterosexual infatuations presently dominating your cinema screens. We shall sculpt statues of beautiful young men, of bold athletes which will be placed in your parks, your squares, your plazas. The museums of the world will be filled only with paintings of graceful, naked lads.

Our writers and artists will make love between men fashionable and *de rigueur,* and we will succeed because we are adept at setting styles. We will eliminate heterosexual liaisons through devices of wit and ridicule, devices which we are skilled at employing.

We will unmask the powerful homosexuals who masquerade as heterosexuals. You will be shocked and frightened when you find that your presidents and their sons, your industrialists, your senators, your mayors, your generals, your athletes, your film stars, your television personalities, your civic leaders, your priests are not the safe, familiar, bourgeois, heterosexual figures you assumed them to be. We are everywhere; we have infiltrated your ranks. Be careful when you speak of homosexuals because we are always among you; we may be sleeping in the same bed with you.

There will be no compromises. We are not middle-class weaklings. Highly intelligent, we are the natural aristocrats of the human race, and steely-minded aristocrats never settle for less. Those who oppose us will be exiled.

We shall raise vast, private armies, as Mishma did, to defeat you. We shall conquer the world because warriors inspired by and banded together by homosexual love and honor are as invincible as were the ancient Greek soldiers.

The family unit—spawning ground of lies, betrayals, mediocrity, hypocrisy, and violence—will be abolished. The family unit, which only dampens imagination and curbs free will, will be eliminated. Perfect boys will be conceived and grown in the genetic laboratory. They will be bonded together in a communal setting, under the control and instruction of homosexual savants.

All churches who condemn us will be closed. Our only gods are handsome young men. We adhere to a cult of beauty, moral and aesthetic. All that is ugly and vulgar and banal will be annihilated. Since we are alienated from middle-class heterosexual conventions, we are free to live our lives according to the dictates of pure imagination. For us too much is not enough.

The exquisite society to emerge will be governed by an elite comprised of gay poets. One of the major requirements for a position of power in the new society of homoeroticism will be indulgence in the Greek passion. Any man contaminated with heterosexual lust will be automatically barred from a position of influence. All males who insist on remaining stupidly heterosexual will be tried in homosexual courts of justice and will become invisible men.

We shall rewrite history, history filled and debased with your heterosexual lies and distortions. We shall portray the homosexuality of great leaders and thinkers who have shaped the world. We will demonstrate that homosexuality and intelligence and imagination are inexorably linked, and that homosexualty is a requirement for true nobility, true beauty in man.

We shall be victorious because we are fueled with the ferocious bitterness of the oppressed who have been forced to play seemingly bit parts in your dumb, heterosexual shows throughout the ages. We too are capable of firing guns and manning the barricades of the ultimate revolution.

Tremble, hetero swine, when we appear before you without our masks.

4. *NFD Journal,* December 1986, 11.

5. *NFD Journal,* May 1987, 5.

6. "The Humane Holocaust," quoted in *Abortion and the Conscience of a Nation,* Ronald Reagan, (New York: Thomas Nelson, 1984), 80-81.

7. Steve Gallagher, *Sexual Idolatry,* (Crittenden, KY: Pure Life Press, 1986).

Chapter 2: The Scriptures and Seduction

1. This comes from part of my experience with my wife as volunteer street-team with Friendship Unlimited, a prostitution alternative outreach in Portland, Oregon.

2. *The Pulpit Commentary,* Vol. XXI (McLean, VA: McDonald Publishing Co.), 12-13.

3. Proverbs 7:15, emphasis added.

4. Proverbs 7:22.

5. 1 Kings 11:4.

6. If repression causes deviancy, then most serial killers and rapists would be from homes of Amish, Mennonite, or other strict groups. This is *not* the case.

7. Barbara Ehrenreich, Elizabeth Hess, and Gloria Jacobs, *Re-Making Love: The Feminization of Sex* (Garden City, New York: Anchor Press/Doubleday, 1986), 119-20.

8. *The Oregonian*, March 15, 1987.

9. Richard Weaver, *Ideas Have Consequences* (Chicago: Univ. of Chicago Press, 1948), 10.

Chapter 3: The Love Connection

1. In my dictionary, one of the archaic definitions for *amuse* was "to begile, delude."

2. Anyone who doubts this needs to try to make such utterly beautiful poetry about their spouse. It requires the exercise of a disciplined imagination and mind to compile such lists of deep and meaningful allegories.

3. William Shakespeare, *Romeo and Juliet,* Act 2, Scene II.

4. "It's Now or Never," Words and music by Aaron Schroeder and Wally Gold, (Gladys Music, 1960), Adapted from an Italian song, "O Solo Mio," lyrics by G. Capurro and

music by Eduardo Capua. RCA records released this as a best seller by Elvis Presley.

5. C. S. Lewis, *The Screwtape Letters*, (New York: Macmillan Publishing, 1980), 21.

Chapter 4: Mr. Natural and the Sexual Revolution

1. The French Revolutionaries literally stripped the church of its ownership of Notre Dame and rechristened it "The Temple of Reason." Allegorically, they stole the achievements of Christianity and claimed them for their own. This sort of thing is common in the humanist movement.

2. "During the French Revolution, the Goddess of Reason presided over a one-year Reign of Terror that saw more people massacred and guillotined (40,000) than were executed in all of the Inquisitions during the Middle Ages." Tom Visoky, "Praise of secularism must be held for history," *The Oregonian*, April 5, 1989, D-7.

3. *Tractacus Theologico-Politicus (1670)*, 7 (Trans. J. Ratner in *The Philosophy of Spinoza*, quoted in *Worlds in Collision* by Immanuel Velikovsky).

4. Apologies to *The American Spectator*.

5. See *The Basic Writings of Sigmund Freud*, translated and edited by Abraham Brill, 1938.

6. A recounting of this "fall from grace" can be found in Francis Schaeffer's *The Great Evangelical Disaster* (Westchester, IL: Crossway Books, 1984).

7. This is not related to the injudicious use of chemicals or forced growth techniques, but it is a plain fact that wild strawberry bushes produce few and tiny berries. No "natural" environment can produce the abundance and the quality of food needed to feed a reasonably sized population.

8. See *The Basic Writings of Sigmund Freud*, translated and edited by Abraham Brill, 1938.

9. Phyllis Grosskurth, *Havelock Ellis: A Biography,* (New York: Alfred A. Knopf, 1980).

10. Justin Kaplan, *Walt Whitman: A Life,* (New York: Bantam Books, 1982), 86-87, 233-40, 281-87.

11. *Pivot of Civilization* (New York: Brentano's, 1922), 271.

12. This admission came from an 86-year-old grandmother who had been one of those girls. She said, "We were just joking. We were just having fun." They had no idea who their visitor was. The hoax is documented in a book by a former supporter of Mead's assertions, Derek Freeman. In his book, *Margaret Mead and Samoa—the Making and Unmaking of an Anthropological Myth,* Freeman reveals the entrenched Samoan moral code that protects virtue with puritanical fervor. The *noble savage* is also obsessed by rank and prone to outbursts of violence and aggression. (Keith Dalton, in *The Oregonian,* November 23, 1988).

13. Cooper's *Last of the Mohicans* and Burrough's *Tarzan of the Apes* are prime examples of the popular genre.

14. I refer here to the Tasaday hoax. For more information see Sharon Begley, "Back from the Stone Age?" *Newsweek,* (May 5, 1986); Bruce Bower, "The Strange Case of the Tasaday" *Science News,* (May 6, 1989); and Bruce Bower, "Tasaday Controversy Grows More Curious," *Science News,* (November 25, 1989).

Chapter 5: Porno Pitfall

1. Radio interview between Margie Boule, Jerry Butler, and the author broadcasted over KXL, Portland, Oregon, August 18, 1989.

2. "The King v. Sedley," 1 Keble 620 (K.B.), 83 Eng. Rep. 1146 (1663).

3. Included in the fantasy of pornography are the excuses for its use. Here I list the most common along with their responses. Note how large a part "love," naturalistic "sci-

ence," and pseudo-sophistication play in them. These excuses are even widely used in Christian circles.

EXCUSE #1: There is nothing wrong with admiring the beauty of nature. The human body is a beautiful creation of God. There is nothing to be ashamed of in the human form. Even Adam and Eve were naked and "not ashamed." Wouldn't it be good if we could get back to that simple state?

ANSWER: Jesus said that those who looked at a woman to lust after her were already committing adultery. There are numerous Old Testament scriptures which prohibit "uncovering the nakedness" of someone other than one's spouse. The reasons for these statements are obvious — human nature is fallen, corrupt, and deceitful. It is foolish to tread into such a hazardous area of the human psyche supposing to attain to the pre-fallen nature of man through one of man's weakest links. If you want to admire nature, look at a tree. If it's the human form you want, buy a mirror!

EXCUSE #2: It is better to look at people making love than pictures of hate and violence.

ANSWER: There is no love in pornography. Women (and everything else) become mere implements of self-gratification. Often force or violence is an integral part of the the scenes of pornography. Men are quickly sated by the simple nude and graduate to more coarse material in due time.

EXCUSE #3: It helps me in my marital relations with my wife.

ANSWER: Pornography not only portrays a degraded view of womanhood and manhood, but it sets an impossible standard for women to live up to. Reality will never be a match for the airbrushed fantasy world of the actors and actresses in front of the camera. Repeated studies have shown that marital dissatisfaction is the most likely result of the use of pornography as a "marital aid."

Most of the "marital aid" claimed is in the form of fantasy. Is it appropriate, however, for a man to fantasize about having sex with a woman in a magazine or film while having relations with his wife? I think not. Consider Christ's warning about "looking at a woman to lust after her."

Beyond this, people begin tc view the kinky practices seen in most pornography as being more common than they are in reality. Counselors who have faced this issue can tell horrifying tales of men insisting that their wives submit to perverse sexual acts under the color of "enhancing the relationship."

EXCUSE #4: It is art.

ANSWER: There are many suitable subjects for art — the privacy of sexuality is not one of them. Honesty demands that we recognize that sexual arousal and gratification are the goal of all such "art."

Actually, pornography is prostitution. Prostitution can be defined as someone selling themselves for the sexual gratification of others. Proverbs is very specific about the dangers of prostitutes, noting that the trouble begins with a look.

Biblically, sexual gratification is only legitimate in the marriage bed.

A corollary to this excuse is that pornography helps to drain off sexual tensions, allowing one to control sinful sexual practices.

First of all, this model, called the satiation or catharsis theory, promotes the un-Biblical view of man as a "bag" of emotions and drives which mysteriously fills to bursting if not allowed to be "vented" in some less harmful way. Second, the theory has been scientifically relegated to the bogus file. Even the theory's originator, Seymore Feshbach, has recanted under his own continued testing of the hypothesis.

EXCUSE #5: I like the articles. There are intellectually stimulating ideas presented in many of these magazines.

ANSWER: There is nothing new under the sun — not even ideas. Any truly worthwhile ideas presented in these publications are sure to find print in less objectionable formats. While it is doubtful that any ideas of eternal consequence would be found in one of these magazines, if such an idea slipped in, I will warrant that it may be easily and more cogently found in the Bible. Meanwhile you are supporting a multibillion dollar, mob-controlled industry which traffics in human bondage, exploitation, and misery.

4. Humor is known to be an effective means of breaking down inhibitions. Molesters of boys often use dirty jokes to gain the confidence of their victims. It binds them both together in a secret pact against the parents and other authorities, and that bond is distinctly sexual because of the nature of the "humor."

5. This sequelae has been verified in dozens of empirical and clinical studies of pornography. The sequence is (1) addiction, (2) escalation, (3) desensitization, and (4) acting out. The steps may occur over a period of years or scant months. With some, the process never reaches some stages, but even the addiction phase alone has enough damaging effects to warrant serious concern.

6. Roth v. United States, 354 U.S. 476 (1957).

7. A later case, Miller v. California 413 U.S. 15 (1973), further defined (and weakened) the *Roth* standard, saying that to be obscene material must meet these conditions:

- The average person, applying contemporary community standards, would find that the work, taken as a whole, appeals to the prurient interest [in sex}; and

- The work depicts or describes, in a patently offensive way, sexual conduct specifically defined in the applicable state [or federal] law; and

- The work, taken as a whole, lacks serious literary, artistic, political, or scientific value.

8. A private contact.

9. It is reported that 70 percent of all pornographic materials ends up in the hands of minors.

10. Dr. Park Deitz, who served on the 1986 President's Commission on Pornography, came to similar conclusions. Deitz began his tenure on that body believing that pornography had no causal relationship to sexual behavior. The evidence changed his mind. (See *Commission Report*, 487-92.)

11. Many of the following assertions are documented in a booklet from Family Policy Insights called, *Pornography and Its Effects on Family, Community, and Culture,* by David Alexander Scott. The conclusions are stated in the text and scrupulously documented from studies and writings of researchers and law enforcement officials. The booklet is the best available and may be obtained for $5 from Family Policy Insights, 721 Second St., N.E., Washington, D.C. 20002, (202) 546-3004. This particular assertion is found on p. 6 of the booklet.

12. In most of this genre of films, the victim is barely concealed behind a shower curtain or being systematically undressed (by herself or a boyfriend) when the violence is introduced.

13. Quoted in Dr. James Dobson, *The Winnable War* (video), Focus on the Family, 1987.

14. David Alexander Scott, *Pornography and Its Effects on Family, Community, and Culture,* 5.

15. Ibid., 4.

16. Ibid., 5.

17. Ibid., 6.

18. Friendship Unlimited, a ministry to prostitutes, reports that prostitutes say that customers often come to them "porn magazine in hand" and point out the acts they want.

19. Dr. Judith Reisman, "Executive Summary: Images of Children, Crime and Violence in *Playboy, Penthouse* and *Hustler* Magazines," 1987. Available for $1 from American Family Association, P. O. Drawer 2440, Tupelo, Mississippi 38803, (601) 844-5036.

20. Linda Lovelace, former star of the porn "classic" *Deep Throat,* now fights pornography and testifies that the film was made through many beatings and at the muzzle of a gun.

21. This industry takes in eight to ten *billion* dollars per year — more than the entire legitimate movie industry. This does not reflect the *number* of customers but the fervency of the addictions. Much of the "legitimate" movie industry panders to the same perversity — though less overtly.

Chapter 6: Fleshpeddlers

1. I deliberately do not use the term "high-class" with call girl. Recent investigations reveal that it is often the same women who work the slimiest streets, who also are on the "call" circuit.

2. When people assert this, I like to ask them if they feel that their own mother was nothing but a career whore with poor business sense. Most are offended at the thought, but continue to parrot the principle.

3. See George Grant, *Grand Illusions,* (Brentwood, TN: Wolgemuth & Hyatt Publishers, Inc., 1988), 53-54, 57, 59.

4. The mockery of morality implicit in the name is intentional. Another sister group is DOLPHIN, or Dump Obsolete Laws; Prove Hypocrisy Isn't Necessary. The names of their literature reflect the same scorn, but the titles would be inappropriate to print.

5. This is a composite of several women we met while working with Friendship Unlimited Inner City Ministries. One of them disappeared and was later identified as a victim of

serial killer, Dayton Leroy Rogers. Another came to the Friendship Center after surviving multiple stab wounds to the chest by a "john." Later, after successfully building a new life with a job and an apartment of her own, she returned to the streets again because she craved "the action."

6. Don't get me wrong! One-sixth is still deplorable, but there are those who have a vested interest in keeping this figure high. Social workers, state-funded outreach agencies, and the kids themselves, who are experts at extracting sympathy, all benefit from the exaggeration. Figures from *Pornography and Its Effects on Family, Community, and Culture,* 18.

7. Ibid., 18.

8. *AFA Journal,* June 1987, 18

9. Robert Berry, "A Market that Feeds Hidden Hunger," *The Atlanta Constitution,* May 1, 1987.

Chapter 7: Sodom Revisited

1. An incident on the street while working with Friendship Unlimited.

2. Michael Swift, *Gay Community News,* and reprinted in the *Congressional Record,* February 15-21, 1987. Full text reprinted in footnotes for chapter 1.

3. *Guide Magazine,* April 1989, 4. In this letter "Father" Thomas goes on to claim that there are two scriptural examples of "gay" marriage and even a psalm in praise of "gay" marriage. He gives no specific citations.

4. I must make an immediate definition of *homosexual.* I refuse to succumb to the modern diversion of distinguishing bi-sexuals from homosexuals. Nor will I spend much time distinguishing between their various peculiar preferences. A homosexual, by my definition, is one who engages in sexual activities with members of his own sex. If they also engage in other types of sex, this definition still holds.

Those who have permanently ceased such activity are excluded from the definition.

5. *Just Out,* June 1989, 2.

6. AIDS Coalition To Unleash Power.

7. Marshall K. Kirk and Erastes Pill, "The Overhauling of Straight America," *Guide Magazine,* November 1987, 7-14.

8. This became the basis for the Gay and Lesbian Pride Day celebrations seen yearly in most large U.S. cities.

9. Henry Klingeman, "Anonymous Sex," *The National Review,* June 19, 1987, 42-43.

10. Kirk and Pill, "The Overhauling of Straight America," p. 8.

11. Pamphlet from Cascade AIDS Project (undated).

12. *San Francisco Chronicle,* November 6, 1987.

13. *The Oregonian,* June 18, 1986.

14. United Press International, April 1987.

15. *The Oregonian,* November 14, 1988.

16. *The Oregonian,* July 3, 1989.

17. *The Oregonian,* May 31, 1989. (The voters later overturned the ordinance.)

18. *AFA Journal,* October 1985, 11-12.

19. People with HIV positive tests for the AIDS virus qualify as "handicapped" under government regulations.

20. Kirk and Pill, "The Overhauling of Straight America."

21. Swift, *Gay Community News.*

22. Alexander Pope, *Essay on Man.*

23. *The Oregonian,* June 8, 1989.

24. The show and quote are real. Billy is an imaginary representative of the millions of unsuspecting little boys who had their minds polluted by that program.

25. Jay and Young, *The Gay Report,* 275. Referred to in *AFA Journal,* February 1988, 10.

26. *AFA Journal,* September 1987, 1.

27. "Gays in the Classroom," *New York Post,* July 5, 1979. Quoted in *AFA Journal,* February 1988, 10.

28. *AFA Journal,* April 1989, 10.

29. R. Halfhill and E. Shamback, "Homophobia and the Berean League Report," *GMPGD,* 1985, 14. In *Are Gay Rights Right?,* Roger Magnuson (Minneapolis, Minnesota: Straitgate Press, 1985), 77.

30. *AFA Journal,* July 1986, 6.

31. *AFA Journal,* June 1985, 3.

Chapter 8: The Modern Mire: Being Led as an Ox

1. From an interview with a fifteen-year-old prostitute in England. In Gitta Sereny, *The Invisible Children: Child Prostitution in America, West Germany, and Great Britain* (New York: Alfred A. Knopf, 1985), 188.

2. Dr. James Dobson's description of what he had seen while serving on The President's Commission on Pornography. *The Winnable War,* Focus on the Family, (1987).

3. Ehrenreich, et.al, *Re-Making Love.*

4. Ibid., 60.

5. Ibid., 2.

6. *AFA Journal,* December 1986, 16.

7. One example is the newspaper ad for the R-rated *Bye Bye Baby* showing the nearly naked Brigitte Nielsen and Carol Alt. The promo line read, "Lisa's a pool shark in paradise with only one problem . . . her boyfriend is her girlfriend's husband."

8. "Knowledge not a contraceptive," *The Oregonian,* December 5, 1986.

9. An ad in a New York newspaper in May 1988.

10. Mary Pride, *All the Way Home* (Westchester, IL: Crossway Books, 1989) 83-84.

11. Ehrenreich, et.al, *Re-Making Love*, 109-111.

12. Ad for Michael Max Leather, *The Village Voice*, May 10, 1988.

13. Frank F. Furstenberg, Jr., sociologist from the University of Pennsylvania, quoted in *The Oregonian*, June 12, 1989.

14. This was the actual advice given in a *Parade* magazine article several years ago. I no longer have the article so I cannot supply the date.

15. Betty Dodson (New York: Harmony Books, 1987). The first printing was in the early seventies.

16. Taken from an article by Ernest Volkman and Howard L. Rosenberg, "The Shame of the Nation," *Family Weekly*, June 2, 1985.

17. *AFA Journal*, June 1985, 6.

18. This was the feature that gained the coveted PG rating for the "children's movie" *E.T.*

19. Scott, *Pornography and Its Effects on Family, Community, and Culture*, 6.

20. *AFA Journal*, July 1989, 14.

21. R. Hazelwood, P. Dietz, and A. Burgess, "The Investigation of Autoerotic Fatalities," *Journal of Police Science and Administration*, September 1981, 404-411.

22. *AFA Journal*, December 1986, 16.

23. Jacqueline Kasun, *Planned Parenthood Sex Education and Mental Health Report*, 1979.

24. "A New Look at Incest," *Forum*, November 1976, 84-89.

25. "A Child's Bill of Rights," *Ms. Magazine*, p. 69.

26. *AFA Journal*, May 1987, 11, 13.

27. *AFA Journal,* January 1986, 18.

Chapter 9: The Church Slips: A Dart in the Liver

1. Erwin W. Lutzer, *How to Say NO to a Stubborn Habit,* (Wheaton, IL: Victor Books, 1982), 23.

2. In the following material, I will quote the work of a number of notable Christian leaders with whom I disagree on specific issues. It is my intention to argue the points themselves and not the personalities. My conflict is with the spirit of the age, not individuals. Let me clearly state here that my comments are in no way to be construed as a judgment on any of these people's intentions or Christian character.

3. Proverbs 17:20b (NAS).

4. Tim and Beverly LaHaye, *The Act of Marriage* (Grand Rapids, MI: Zondervan, 1976), 267.

5. Thanks to Daniel Davis.

6. From an interview with the author. Sam's name was changed.

7. For excellent Biblical work on the Onan story in both Catholic and Protestant teaching, see Charles D. Provan, *The Bible and Birth Control,* (Monongahela, PA: Zimmer Printing, 1989).

8. Jackie Scott, "Christian Press Thrives on Today's Issues," *The Oregonian,* August 13, 1985. Second Timothy 4:3 warns that in the last days people will "heap to themselves teachers, having itching ears."

9. Randy Alcorn, *Christians in the Wake of the Sexual Revolution,* (Multnomah Press, 1985).

10. Tim and Beverly LaHaye, *The Act of Marriage* (Grand Rapids, MI: Zondervan, 1976), 268-72.

11. This statement was directly quoted and cited in *A Gift for All Ages,* Clifford and Joyce Penner (Waco, Texas: Word Books, 1986), 156.

12. "The War Within," *Fulness Magazine* (date unknown). Reprinted from *Leadership* magazine (Fall 1982).

13. Ehrenreich, et.al, *Re-Making Love*, 144.

14. Romans 12:2, NAS.

15. Ehrenreich, et.al, *Re-Making Love*, 145.

16. In *Re-Making Love,* the authors play a double entendre between the Second Coming of Christ and the second "coming" as a gutteral reference to sexual climax. In another case they say, "[Christian women] dream of a love affair with Christ" which would be utterly despicable except that they show where "Christian" authors recommend this kind of fantasy.

17. Dr. Ed and Gaye Wheat, *Intended For Pleasure,* (Old Tappan, NJ: Fleming H. Revell, 1977, revised 1981), 23.

18. Ibid., 30.

19. Ibid., 22.

20. Rev. Tim and Beverly LaHaye also propound that a wife has a "right to expect to be loved to orgasm." *The Act of Marriage,* 268.

21. From an interview with the author. Sandra is a ficticious name.

22. Ehrenreich, et.al, *Re-Making Love*, 150.

23. LaHaye, *The Act of Marriage.*

24. Charles and Martha Shedd, *Celebration in the Bedroom,* (Waco, Texas: Word Books, 1979).

25. Ibid., 114-115. On pages 29 and 30, neither author could bring himself to come out against sadism, transvestitism, and bondage—within marriage of course. They retreated into a kind of "who are we to say what is normal" argument

26. From transcript of "Donahue" number 03082, Multimedia Program Productions, Cincinnati, OH. Obtained through

Journal Graphics Inc., 267 Broadway, New York, NY 10007.

27. Mary Pride, *The Way Home,* (Westchester, IL: Crossway Books 1985).

28. Mary Pride, *All the Way Home,* (Westchester, IL: Crossway Books 1989).

29. *Guide Magazine,* April 1989, 4.

30. Tony Campolo, *20 Hot Potatoes Christians are Afraid to Touch* (Waco, TX: Word Books, 1988), 112.

Chapter 10: God, Marriage, and Sex: Throwing off the Shackles

1. Mary Pride, *The Way Home* (Westchester, IL: Crossway Books, 1985), 40.

2. Matthew 19:9 and 1 Corinthians 7:15. The best exposition I have heard to date on this subject was the tape series, *Jesus' Teaching on Divorce,* by Pastor John MacArthur of Grace Community Church.

3. Genesis 2:20b NAS.

4. Revelation 4:11.

5. Malachi 2:15 NIV.

6. *Interlinear Greek-English New Testament,* George Ricker Berry, Ph.D., ed. (Grand Rapids, MI: Zondervan, 1971).

7. The Episcopal Church.

8. Mary Pride, *The Way Home,* 26.

9. Mary Pride, *All the Way Home,* (Westchester, IL: Crossway Books, 1989).

10. Available from Home Life, P. O. Box 1250, Fenton, MO 63026 for $15.

11. Proverbs 18:22 NAS.

Chapter 11: A Christian America, A Christian West, A Christian World: Spreading the Freedom

1. Matthew 28:19-20 NAS.

2. Ezekiel 3:17-21.

3. Sam eventually did his Master's thesis on temptation and discovered the prescription in James: (1) Scripture, (2) prayer, (3) resistance, and (4) wisdom, or the Holy Spirit.

4. From the introduction to *Sexual Idolatry* (1986).

5. Romans 3:4 NAS.

6. Matthew 5:29 NAS, emphasis added.

7. James 4:7 KJV.

8. John 8:31 NAS, emphasis added.

9. Exodus 34:11-12 NAS.

10. Joshua 17:13.

11. For years, I took no action against abortion and pornography though I knew their deep destructiveness and wickedness. These abominations have escalated in part because I and others like me were too pietistic.

12. Psalm 127:4–5 NAS.

13. Franky Schaeffer, *Bad News for Modern Man* (Westchester, IL: Crossway Books 1984), 135–36.

14. Connie Marshner, *Decent Exposure: How to Teach Your Children about Sex* (Brentwood, TN: Wolgemuth & Hyatt, 1988), 19.

15. 1 Kings 19:1-21.

16. Isaiah 51:9a NAS.

INDEX

abortion, 15, 101, 105, 154, 174, 208, 221–222
ACLU, 88, 127
addiction, sexual, 14, 39, 81–82, 89–90, 93,175–177
adultery, 15
advertising industry, 10–11, 18–19, 91, 145–146, 148–149, 158–159, 172
AIDS, 124–125,127–128, 155, 159
American Psychiatric Association (APA), 124, 134
Amsterdam, 108
amusement, 49–50
anal sex, 180, 191
arranged marriage, 60, 211–212
auto-erotic fatalities, 159–160

Babylon, 11, 14, 91
bait-and-switch, 10–11, 19, 22, 73, 129–134
Bakker, Jim and Tammi, 37
Bathsheba, 28–30, 35
birth control, 101, 103, 154, 184, 202, 203, 204, 207–208, 211
bondage and discipline (B&D), 39, 90
Bundy, Ted, 6–8
Butler, Jerry, 81–82

Campolo, Tony, 193
Catharsis Theory, 93
Chasteline De Vergi, 54
Chaucer, 59
child porn, 86, 93, 94, 147–148, 157–159, 162

ABOUT THE AUTHOR

Paul deParrie is a pro-family, pro-life activist. A father of six, he is a former pastor, street minister to prostitutes, and director of an antipornography group. He is the author of *The Rescuers* (Wolgemuth and Hyatt, 1989) and co-author with Mary Pride of *Unholy Sacrifices of the New Age* (Crossway Books, 1988) and *Ancient Empires of the New Age* (Crossway Books, 1989).

Mr. deParrie lives in Portland, Oregon, with his wife, Bonnie, and his children, Djinn, Joshua, Jeanne, Yvonne, Michelle, and Nicole.

The typeface for the text of this book is *Times Roman*. In 1930, typographer Stanley Morison joined the staff of *The Times* (London) to supervise design of a typeface for the reformatting of this renowned English daily. Morison had overseen type-library reforms at Cambridge University Press in 1925, but this new task would prove a formidable challenge despite a decade of experience in paleography, calligraphy, and typography. *Times New Roman* was credited as coming from Morison's original pencil renderings in the first years of the 1930s, but the typeface went through numerous changes under the scrutiny of a critical committee of dissatisfied *Times* staffers and editors. The resulting typeface, *Times Roman*, has been called the most used, most successful typeface of this century. The design is of enduring value to English and American printers and publishers, who choose the typeface for its readability and economy when run on today's high-speed presses.

Substantive Editing:
Michael Hyatt

Copy Editing:
Susan Kirby

Cover Design:
Steve Diggs & Friends
Nashville, Tennessee

Page Composition:
Xerox Ventura Publisher
Printware 720 IQ Laser Printer

Printing and Binding:
Maple-Vail Book Manufacturing Group,
York, Pennsylvania

Cover Printing:
Weber Graphics
Chicago, Illinois